Jackie K

The Widow of Camelot

By Michael W. Simmons

Table of Contents

Introduction

"When you get written about a lot, you just think of it as a little cartoon that runs along at the bottom of your life—but one that doesn't have much to do with your life."

—Jacqueline Kennedy Onassis

In the minds of many people, Jackie Kennedy is still the woman they think of when they imagine what the ideal First Lady ought to be. She was young, beautiful, aristocratic in a uniquely American way, and while she was First Lady, she tended to enjoy greater popularity with the American people than her own husband.

But how to explain her enduring popularity, and her now iconic status in American history? Many

First Ladies have been attractive, stylish, and graceful, after all. These qualities have long been considered prerequisites in the wife of any high-level male politician, which makes it hardly surprising when they turn up in the possession of the wife of an American president.

Yet no other First Lady has ever been thrust into the starring role in one of the most legendary tragedies of modern American history the way that Jackie Kennedy was. The assassination of John F. Kennedy effectively eclipsed everything that Jackie Kennedy had accomplished in her role in the White House before it. While her husband was alive, she redefined the role of the President's wife by turning the White House into the living museum of American history that it is today. Intelligent, well-educated, and possessing a keen interest in history and knowledge of antiquities, Jackie Kennedy had recognized that she was uniquely placed to act as a steward and conservator of her country's legacy by curating the collection of art and artifacts that had always resided in the White House, yet had never before been displayed to the best possible effect. Even if it had not been for the events of November 22, 1963, she would deserve to be remembered by history as one of the most uniquely capable First Ladies the office of the President has ever known.

It would no doubt surprise many people today to know that the Kennedys—both of them—were frequently just as beset by criticism from a disapproving American public as any of the most beleaguered presidents of recent decades. Even Jackie's White House renovation project came under fire from people who misunderstood both her intentions, and the manner in which governmental funds are allocated.

Jackie was never entirely comfortable being so much in the public eye, and she felt tremendous guilt whenever any action of hers, however innocent, caused embarrassment for her husband's administration. Many of the qualities for which she is now venerated—her chic fashion sense, her ability to charm crowds with her shy, retiring, yet gracious manner—struck Americans in the early 1960s as too rarefied, too snobbish, to be appropriate in a president's wife. But Jackie's keen sense for managing the outward appearance of things would serve her well in the days and weeks following Kennedy's assassination. It informed all her decisions, and enabled her to put aside her own grief and shock to lead the nation, and indeed the entire world, in a deeply cathartic and obscurely necessary ritual of mourning for their fallen president.

In the history of the United States, four sitting presidents have been assassinated. The first was Abraham Lincoln, shot by John Wilkes Booth in 1863, shortly after the end of the Civil War. The second was James Garfield, who was shot eighteen years later in 1881 by Charles J. Guiteau. The third was William McKinley, who was shot by Leon Czolgosz twenty years after Garfield, in 1901.

Of these four presidents, only Lincoln and Kennedy, who were both shot in the head, died of their wounds quickly. Garfield and McKinley, who were shot in the back and in the abdomen respectively, survived their initial attacks—Garfield lived for eleven weeks and seemed poised to make a recovery before succumbing to infection, while McKinley lived for seven days. Lincoln, by contrast, lived for only nine hours after being shot in the back of the head, and because of the slow rate at which news traveled in the 19th century, he had expired long before most people even knew of the attack. Kennedy, likewise, was declared dead within an hour of being shot by Lee Harvey Oswald.

Much has been made of coincidental similarities between the lives and deaths of Abraham Lincoln and John F. Kennedy, but the one thing that they share indisputably is the fact that the story of how they died is one that most Americans, even children, know by heart. Virtually everyone knows that Lincoln was shot in the back of the head by John Wilkes Booth while sitting next to his wife in his theater box, watching a play. And most Americans, even those who were not yet born when Kennedy was president, have seen images from the famous Zapruder film: the President and his wife riding in an open convertible, Jackie in her blood-spattered pink suit scrambling over the back of the car to help the Secret Service agent climb inside. Perhaps the reason we remember Lincoln and Kennedy with so much clarity, when history has all but effaced Garfield and McKinley, is due in part to the suddenness of Lincoln and Kennedy's deaths. After all, an assassination attempt against a president is traumatic in itself, even it if is not successful, as the 1981 attempt on the life of

President Ronald Reagan demonstrated. But an assassination ending in instant death and the loss of the president is a double assault on public feeling. Perhaps part of the reason that Garfield and McKinley's deaths no longer haunt us is because there was time, afterwards—time for them to say goodbye to loved ones, to make arrangements for their succession, and for the public to process what had transpired, before they finally slipped away.

Yet this explanation is only partly satisfying. McKinley and Garfield were scarcely memorable as American presidents go; even the shocking manner of their deaths did not save them from relative obscurity. Lincoln and Kennedy are a different matter. We needn't plumb too deeply into why Lincoln's death is still felt as a wound on the American psyche. He was, by any estimation, one of the greatest presidents ever to be elected in the United States. Yet, while Americans consistently rank John F. Kennedy as one of the greatest of all American presidents in popular polls, there is scarcely the same degree of consensus amongst historians. Kennedy held office for slightly less than three years, and during that time his administration was plagued by scandals, both momentous and banal. The Bay of Pigs fiasco is considered a blot on his record, and though his adept handling of the Cuban Missile Crisis garnered praise, it was in part precipitated by Kennedy's poor performance in his 1961 Vienna negotiations with Nikita Khrushchev. Kennedy is widely regarded as one of the most telegenic presidents in American history, and he was undoubtedly a brilliant speaker and campaigner. But his administration made few advances in domestic policy, and though he was sympathetic to the Civil Rights movement, he is not entirely deserving of the credit he often receives for working to advance it.

Compared to the profoundly gifted Abraham Lincoln, who shepherded the nation through the

Civil War and rammed the Thirteenth Amendment down the throats of Congress by wedding political savvy to moral certitude, Kennedy accomplished comparatively little. So why are the names of both men often spoken in the same breath? Why is their loss to the country valued on equal terms?

The significance of the fact that Kennedy's assassination was filmed, and subsequently viewed in all its horrific, brutal detail by millions of people, is undoubtedly responsible for much of the impact that his death had, and continues to have, on the nation. Rarely do sane, moral people seek out or willingly view footage of such brutal violence against another human being. Yet the Zapruder film is viewed by high school students in their history classrooms and by casual television viewers with a taste for historical documentaries. Each of the millions of people who have viewed the film of the assassination have become, in effect, witnesses to it—and to witness a traumatic event is to become traumatized oneself, to a greater or lesser degree. The grief inspired by the Kennedy assassination probably will not recede entirely until people cease viewing that film, and it is probably safe to say that people will never stop viewing it for so long as the footage exists. In an age of digital media, it is possible that the death of John F. Kennedy will continue to serve as a dull ache in the American consciousness for many years to come.

What is a person to do with the pain they feel over the death of a man they never knew, a man who died decades before they were born? The answer is the same as with any death: they grieve, and they search for appropriate ways to mourn. But the truly extraordinary thing about our public mourning for Jack Kennedy is that we still observe the same rituals of grief that were choreographed for our benefit 54 years ago by his widow, Jackie Kennedy.

Not unlike some great queen of the medieval era, Jackie curated the symbols, the rituals, and, crucially in the television age, the images that everyone now associates with Kennedy's death. And in a very real way, she also defined his legacy. The fact of the matter is that we remember John F. Kennedy today, not so much as he was, but as Jackie Kennedy chose that we should remember him. Her role in defining his legacy was largely invisible to the public in the 1960s and for many decades after. The extent to which Jackie shaped our communal memory of her husband has only become apparent more recently, in an era where the contributions of women in history are evaluated more seriously.

The Zapruder film had no director. It is an open eye fixed on a gruesome spectacle. The movements of the actors involved were not scripted. Jackie, fated to be star of the gruesome pageant, was acting on shock and instinct when she tried to pull Kennedy down after the first bullet struck him, and when she reached, blindly, for the piece of skull that exploded from the back of her husband's head after the second bullet found its mark. A slim figure in Chanel pink, she is the sole person springing into immediate action, while the men in dark suits who surround her appear to be slower to react. Dramatically, she climbs over the back of the vehicle and grasps the hand of a Secret Service agent who couldn't quite catch up to the car after the motorcade began to put on speed. It was a scene never meant to be viewed by anyone who wasn't present in Dallas that day. But what came afterwards is a different story.

Jackie refused to change out of her clothes, though they were spattered with her husband's blood and brain matter, until the plane bearing Kennedy's body touched down at Andrews Air Force base. It was important, she felt, that Americans see her as she was at the moment they lost their president, gore and all. In doing so, Jackie transformed herself into an avatar for the nation's grief: with her image before their eyes, every person watching her could imagine themselves in her place, and could thus participate in her mourning for the president.

Every aspect of Kennedy's elaborate funeral, from the riderless black horse that led the procession, to 3-year old John Kennedy saluting his father's coffin, to the eternal flame that burns next to his grave in Arlington, was arranged by Jackie, who, though she was no longer First Lady, was becoming something even more enduring: the black-veiled widow, like Queen Victoria in mourning for Albert, a near-saintly icon of uxorial and maternal virtue. So long as Jackie endured, living in modest retirement as she cared for and protected her two children, the nation's loss was not total. Some part of their martyred president lived on through her.

This was precisely what Jackie intended. Alive to the power of symbols in a way that only a true student of history can be, her parting gift to Kennedy was something he never would have admitted that he wanted. Jackie believed that Kennedy's character had been forged during the long periods he was confined to his sickbed as a child, with nothing to do except read books about history and its great heroes. He had wanted to be another Churchill—or perhaps even King Arthur. He had aspired to that sort of legendary status. Opinions are divided as to whether Kennedy's presidency merits that degree of veneration. But Jackie gave it to him anyway—and she did it by telling the American people a story.

About two weeks after Kennedy's death, on December 6, 1963, journalist Theodore H. White sat down with Jackie for a brief interview. Initially rejected by White's editors at *Life* magazine as too sentimental, Jackie was adamant: if they wanted a story from her, this was the story they were going to get.

She remembers how hot the sun was in Dallas, and the crowds—greater and wilder than the crowds in Mexico or in Vienna. The sun was blinding, streaming down; yet she could not put on sunglasses for she had to wave to the crowd.

And up ahead she remembers seeing a tunnel around a turn and thinking that there would be a moment of coolness under the tunnel. There was the sound of the motorcycles, as always in a parade, and the occasional backfire of a motorcycle. The sound of the shot came, at that moment, like the sound of a backfire and she remembers Connally saying, "No, no, no, no, no..."

She remembers the roses. Three times that day in Texas they had been greeted with the bouquets of yellow roses of Texas. Only, in Dallas, they had given her *red* roses. She remembers thinking, how funny—red roses for me; and then the car was full of blood and red roses.

Much later, accompanying the body from the Dallas hospital to the airport, she was alone with Clint Hill—the first Secret Service man to come to their rescue— and with Dr. Burkley, the White House physician. Burkley gave her two roses that had slipped under the President's shirt when he fell, his head in her lap.

All through the night they tried to separate him from her, to sedate her, and take care of her—and she would not let them. She wanted to be with him...

There was a thought, too, that was always with her. "When Jack quoted something, it was usually classical," she said, "but I'm so ashamed of myself—all I keep thinking of is this line from a musical comedy.

"At night, before we'd go to sleep, Jack liked to play some records; and the song he loved most came at the very end of this record. The lines he loved to hear were: *Don't let it be forgot, that once there was a spot, for one brief shining moment that was known as Camelot.*"

She wanted to make sure that the point came clear and went on: "There'll be great Presidents again—and the Johnsons are wonderful, they've been wonderful to me—but there'll never be another Camelot again.

"Once, the more I read of history the more bitter I got. For a while I thought history was something that bitter old men wrote. But then I realized history made Jack what he was. You must think of him as this little boy, sick so much of the time, reading in bed, reading history, reading the Knights of the Round Table, reading Marlborough. For Jack, history was full of heroes. And if it made him this way—if it made him see the heroes—maybe other little boys will see. Men are such a combination of good and bad. Jack had this hero idea of history, the idealistic view."

But she came back to the idea that transfixed her: *"Don't let it be forgot, that once there was a spot, for one brief shining moment that was known as Camelot*—and it will never be that way again."

As for herself? She was horrified by the stories that she might live abroad. "I'm *never* going to live in Europe. I'm not going to 'travel extensively abroad.' That's a desecration. I'm going to live in the places I lived with Jack. In Georgetown, and with the Kennedys at the Cape. They're my family. I'm going to bring up my children. I want John to grow up to be a good boy."

As for the President's memorial, at first she remembered that, in every speech in their last days in Texas, he had spoken of how in December this nation would loft the largest rocket booster yet into the sky, making us first in space. So she had wanted something of his there when it went up—perhaps only his initials painted on a tiny corner of the great Saturn, where no one need even notice it. But now Americans will seek the moon from Cape Kennedy. The new name, born of her frail hope, came as a surprise.

The only thing she knew she must have for him

was the eternal flame over his grave at Arlington.

"Whenever you drive across the bridge from Washington into Virginia," she said, "you see the Lee Mansion on the side of the hill in the distance. When Caroline was very little, the mansion was one of the first things she learned to recognize. Now, at night, you can see his flame beneath the mansion for miles away."

She said it is time people paid attention to the new President and the new First Lady. But she does not want them to forget John F. Kennedy or read of him only in dusty or bitter histories:

For one brief shining moment there was Camelot.

To say that this is a gilded vision of President Kennedy and his White House is putting it mildly. Far from a King Arthur who had eyes only for his Queen Guinevere, Kennedy was compulsively promiscuous, to a degree that shocked even some of his closest friends. He had trysts with women in Jackie's own bed and in his children's schoolroom. Drug use, sex workers, mistresses, and other illicit indulgences were so common in the Kennedy White House that one of the Kennedys' closest friends asserted that he'd "made that place into a brothel". Nor was Jackie the deceived wife, too naïve to discover the truth of her older husband's wayward habits. She knew what was happening, knew that she was powerless to stop it, and fretted lest Jack's lack of discretion lead to a scandal that would be impossible to cover up, as nearly became the case after Marilyn Monroe's breathless rendition of "Happy Birthday, Mr. President" focused journalistic attention on the rumors of Kennedy's many affairs.

Yet despite all of this, she was fiercely, almost unreasonably loyal to Jack in life. And in death, she quietly drew a veil over the deep unhappiness she had felt for much of their marriage. She came of a time and a class where appearances mattered more than anything. "For Jack, history was full of heroes," she'd told White. "And if it made him this way—if it made him see the heroes—maybe other little boys will see." Jackie may have been one of only a very few people who saw the living Kennedy as a hero. He is remembered as one, by millions of people—but that is because Jackie made people see him that way. She did it for him, and she did it, as she told White, for "other little boys". In other words, for the American people, who needed a heroic image to cling to in the midst of their uncertainty.

The White interview was one of very few interviews Jackie ever gave in which she spoke about the events of November 22, 1963. Long before the assassination of her beloved brother in law, Robert F. Kennedy, in 1968, she had ceased to speak publically of the assassination. Having done her best to etch in marble her version of the history she'd lived through, she seemed to want to leave it alone afterwards, without making any of the re-appraisals or emendations that hindsight might have bestowed.

The history of John F. Kennedy's presidency will continue to be weighed by scholars and academics. But the *story* of his presidency—the enduring legend, the myth of the American Camelot—is still the story that Jackie Kennedy told over 50 years ago. It will never change and never vanish from public memory, because is a fiction, and as such, not subject to any standard of historical truth.

Keen student of history that Jackie was, perhaps she realized that she could achieve in a three hour interview with Theodore H. White what thousands of years of storytelling had achieved for the nameless Briton who inspired the legend of King Arthur. All the history that has ever been written tells the story of at least two people—the story of the person it is written about, and the story of the person writing it. The legend of John F. Kennedy as created by Jackie Kennedy Onassis tells us little about the man, but it tells us a great deal about Jackie as she was in late 1963, a grieving 34-year old widow. The young Jackie Kennedy was an idealist who believed in heroes even more, perhaps, than the little boy her husband used to be, who had once lain in his sickbed dreaming of them. Perhaps the assassination should have shattered that belief; perhaps not. After all, heroes usually die young, in the stories.

Jackie would live for another 31 years after the assassination. By the time she died of cancer in 1994, she had a different perspective on heroes, and on her husband. But she had long ago given up writing other people's stories. She'd had her own life to live.

Chapter One: The Schoolgirl

Jacqueline of the Bouviers

What does it mean to be an American aristocrat—one of the elite, in a society that likes to think of itself as having transcended class barriers? A person searching for the answer to that question could scarcely do better than to examine the early life of former First Lady Jacqueline Kennedy Onassis, born July 28, 1929, to socialite Janet Norton Lee and Wall Street stockbroker John "Black Jack" Bouvier.

Despite being born at the beginning of the Great Depression, Jackie and her sister Lee, four years her junior, enjoyed great privilege during their childhoods. Many of Jack Bouvier's colleagues were ruined by the Black Friday crash of 1929, but Jack managed to keep the bulk of his fortune intact, at least initially. The family was able to keep up appearances, maintaining both their primary residence, a large apartment in Manhattan, and their summer vacation home on Long Island, called Lasata. Yet their marriage fell under strain early on, due in part to mounting financial pressures, and in greater part to Jack Bouvier's many extramarital affairs. The marriage finally foundered in 1936, when Jackie was seven; Janet and Jack separated, and by 1940 they were divorced.

Divorce was uncommon in the social circles that the Bouviers moved in, and the scandal was all the greater because the family was Catholic. When Janet Bouvier remarried in 1942, it was to Hugh D. Auchincloss, who was not merely Protestant, but a scion of upper class Wasp society. His maternal grandfather, Oliver Jennings, had helped found Standard Oil alongside John D. Rockefeller; with such deep wells to draw from, Auchincloss, who like

Bouvier was a stock broker, managed to weather the Depression virtually unscathed.

The marriage was a good match for Janet, and it provided her daughters with promising social connections that would help them both to make good marriages with wealthy young men. But because Auchincloss had three children of his own from two previous marriages, and would go on to have more children with Janet, Jackie and Lee could not expect to inherit anything from him after his death. They were supported at their elite boarding school by Jack Bouvier, who had resented their mother's demands for financial support after their divorce, but began to sing a different tune after her marriage to Auchincloss. It was now a point of pride with him that he, not their wealthy stepfather, paid the girls' tuition and provided them with a small allowance. The Bouvier girls were not heiresses, but they were both deemed great beauties, and Jackie in particular was considered very intelligent. They would never feel quite as secure as their wealthier peers, but their prospects for the future seemed very good. For a young woman in the 1940's, everything depended on making the right sort of marriage, and a pretty girl with cultured manners and a wealthy stepfather was likely to make a very good marriage indeed.

As Jackie grew up, she came into possession of a certain air that set her apart from her peers and gave her a distinct advantage in the matrimonial lists. She was pretty, but she was far from being considered the most beautiful girl of her year— her eyes were thought to be too far apart, and she was said to have strangely large hands. But people swiftly forgot this once they had been talking to Jackie for a few minutes. She had extraordinary social talents, and the kind of charisma that allowed her to command a room with seemingly little effort. Her privileged upbringing undoubtedly helped bring these qualities out in her, but the indefinable "something" in her manners that so many people remarked upon was probably due to the strong sense of aristocratic identity that Jack Bouvier had inculcated in his eldest daughter since she was a small girl.

Jack Bouvier subscribed to his own father's mistaken belief that the Bouvier family was descended from French nobility who had been forced to flee France in 1815, after the Napoleonic Wars. This was, not, in fact, the case at all. Michel Bouvier, the first member of his family to settle in the New World, was no exiled nobleman, but an immigrant craftsman who was destined to live out the fabled self-made American success story. Michel had made his living as a handyman in Philadelphia when he first arrived in the country, eventually saving enough money to move into the furniture manufacturing business. Eventually, he founded the family fortune through successful land speculation. This constituted a considerable rise in the family's circumstances, as the French Bouviers had been "drapers, tailors, glovers, farmers, and even domestic servants". It has even been pointed out that the name "Bouvier" means "cow-herd", which certainly denotes less than aristocratic origins.

Yet Jack Bouvier and his daughter Jackie clung to the myth of their family's noble descent, and these beliefs fostered Jackie's sense that she was destined for some sort of higher calling. Spurious family legends laying claim to elevated European ancestry were not uncommon amongst wealthy American families, but their veracity was virtually beside the point. Most of the people that Jackie associated were also the grandchildren or great-grandchildren of lowly immigrants who had changed their family's fortunes when they changed continents. What mattered more was the effect that Jackie's belief in her aristocratic ancestry had upon her imagination. It led to her develop a passionate interest in France and

French history, which in turn would inspire several trips to post-war Europe when she was a young adult, exposing her to a way of life that differed vastly from anything she had known during her sheltered childhood. As a child growing up during World War II, Jackie avidly followed radio news broadcasts about Nazi-occupied France and the heroic efforts of the French Resistance, led by Charles de Gaulle. He became a personal hero of Jackie's, along with British wartime prime minister Winston Churchill. (Jackie named her dog "Gaullie", in de Gaulle's honor.)

In the uppermost tiers of American society, bloodlines going back more than two or three generations were far less important than money, connections, and appearances. Jackie Bouvier was born to a certain amount of money, and her mother's second marriage provided her with connections. But Jackie possessed a crucial talent for cultivating appearances that was entirely her own.

Her aloof, yet gracious air was also due in part to the effect that her parents' divorce had on her as a child. She was seven when they separated, eleven when they divorced, and thirteen when her mother remarried. In the 1940's, domestic upheaval of this sort set a child apart from her peers in a way that is difficult to appreciate in the 21st century, when divorce is commonplace. Divorces inevitably have a profound effect upon young children, though this was not well understood when Jackie was a child. Her family told themselves that Jackie and her sister were too young to really understand what was happening, much less be affected by it. This may well have been true of Lee, who was only three when her father left the family and would have possessed few memories of their life together as a family of four. But Jackie was older, and she was keenly sensitive to the changes taking place in her life.

People who knew her as a child said that the divorce made Jackie quiet, inward, and watchful. The rarity of divorce amongst the upper classes made it a subject fit for newspaper headlines. "Society Broker Sued for Divorce" was the title of the story that appeared in the society pages after Janet and Jack agreed to formalize the dissolution of their marriage. A photograph of the Bouvier family was published in the newspaper along with the story, and though this was not the first time Jackie's picture had appeared in the papers—she and her mother were both first-rate equestriennes whose accomplishments on horseback had been reported upon in the society pages in the past— the attention it brought down on her was of a very different sort than she had been used to. Her classmates at her day school mocked her viciously. In the words of one biographer, Jackie "reacted to the publicity as if she had been flayed alive". She was an object of ridicule at school, and at home, she became so guarded as to be considered unreadable.

Jackie's cousin, John H. Davis, who would go on to write a history of their family, described the young Jackie as having a "tendency to withdraw frequently into a private world of her own." Outwardly, she seemed to be an easy child, obedient and willing to conform to expectations, but she also possessed a "fiercely independent inner life" which enabled her to develop strong, original opinions, a keen sense of judgment, and a will of her own. Still waters ran deep, where Jackie was concerned. Her teachers at school found her intelligent and charming, but she was also capable of creating startling disruptions in the classroom. Jackie was generally well-behaved, but she was not meek, and as she grew older she was anything but an empty vessel for other people's ambitions. Davis writes that she "possessed a mysterious authority, even as a teen-ager, that would compel people to do her bidding." In small groups, when there were only one or two people around, she kept her thoughts to herself. But when she was in larger gatherings, she seemed to come into her own, effortlessly taking command of the room and "dazzling people" with displays of charm and wit. She was a born performer with an extraordinary sense of occasion—self-sufficient, yet not shy, comfortable when taking center stage. But her inner thoughts and feelings remained closely guarded.

The most popular girl in Newport

Jackie's social talents first began to emerge a few years after her mother Janet married Hugh Auchincloss and moved with her daughters to Newport, Rhode Island. In these new surroundings, Jackie was, in her own words, "petrified of everything"—at least at first. But by 1945, when she was sixteen, she had become far more confident, and was fully prepared to start undertaking more adult social responsibilities. In other words, she was beginning to think seriously about marriage. Sixteen was not old enough to marry, but in the same way that motivated young people today start preparing for college in their sophomore or junior year of high school, teenage girls in Jackie's world attended teas, dances, and afternoon cocktail parties in the knowledge that the relationships they formed as school girls would set the course for their adult lives. The cocktail party circuit in Newport existed specifically to introduce eligible young men to suitable young women of their own social class, and thus it was, in the summer of 1945, that Jackie met the young man who would become her first boyfriend—a Harvard student named Bev, some four years older than her.

When Jackie Bouvier was young, the entire purpose of a woman's education was to prepare her for married life. If she was studious, with a serious interest in history, politics, and current events, as Jackie was, it was seen as a potential asset to her future husband, since she could more easily converse with and entertain his guests and business associates. But it would not do for her to be seen as too clever, or to be pursuing academic achievement for its own sake. The prevailing wisdom of the day was that, to attract a husband, a girl should "seem bright enough to interest a man but not so bright as to imperil his ego".

Jackie performed her social duties in the manner expected of her, though they often required her to censor herself during conversations with preening young Ivy Leaguers who were trying to impress her. Jackie accepted the necessity of holding her tongue on her such occasions, but catering to the egos of so many mediocre young men grated on her nerves from time to time. At one of her stepfather's cocktail parties, Jackie found herself cornered by an earnest young man who wanted to lecture her about Phillipe Pétain and Vichy rule in France during the second World War. Jackie, of course, knew far more about Pétain than he did. But she nodded and smiled nonetheless while the boy prattled on, not expressing any frustration until she was alone with her friend afterwards: "He sounded like a little boy who's just read a big book and is having a lovely time expounding it all to a little country urchin without really knowing what it was all about. I wanted to give him a big maternal kiss on the cheek and tell him he was really a big boy now!"

Jackie made her mark on Newport society in the summer of 1945. She would never be an Auchincloss, or heiress to any of the Standard Oil wealth that came with the name, but she was the sort of step-daughter that an Auchincloss could be proud to introduce as a member of the family. Her popularity was helped along by the fact that she was a new face, something rarely seen in the insular circles of the elite. Two young men who had made Jackie's acquaintance over that summer asked whether they might write to her when they returned to Harvard, and the practical Jackie could only agree. After all, both boys were eligible matrimonial prospects in their different ways. But she found the labor of being courted tedious. The two boys knew each other and were members of the same club at Harvard, so she had to write separate, original replies to both their letters, though one reply copied twice would have suited her better. To hold their interest, Jackie challenged herself to be "devastatingly witty", but she chose safe subjects for her witticisms. Chiefly, she complained about her school, Miss Porter's, and Farmington, the quiet, boring New England town where Miss Porter's was located. Her complaints about school life were certainly sincere enough. Jackie was feeling constrained and under-stimulated by life in "prison," as she called it, and in one letter, she remarked that, "If schooldays are the happiest days of your life, I'm hanging myself with my skip-rope tonight."

Miss Porter's School is one of the oldest and most famous boarding schools for young women in the United States. Nowadays, it has a reputation for academic rigor, and even when Jackie was a student there, more and more graduates were going on to college. But most people in Jackie's life considered Miss Porter's little more than a finishing school—one of those now virtually extinct institutions in which wealthy young women were taught social graces in a safely cloistered environment while they matured into readiness for matrimony. Seniors on the verge of graduating from Miss Porter's generally expected to have a debutante season, swiftly followed by an engagement to an eligible young man, then marriage within a year or two of having left school. Accordingly, it seemed to most people that Jackie's future was already settled by the end her senior year. She had formed a serious relationship with one of the two Harvard boys she'd met in Newport in 1945, and the two were regarded as a couple. Marriage within a year or so was the normal and expected course for their relationship. Jackie would leave school and be presented to society around the same time that her boyfriend was graduating from Harvard and getting his start in the business world. By the time Jackie had joined the junior committees of a few charitable organizations and danced at a few balls, it would be time for her to become a wife.

This first boyfriend of Jackie's was named Bev. He was good looking, sweet, and able to make Jackie laugh; but for awhile, he'd had a rival named John, who was less handsome but wrote brilliant, interesting letters, and fascinated Jackie with his intelligence. The problem with John was that the idea of kissing him made

Jackie want to gag, as she confided to a school friend. Bev, on the other hand, she wanted to kiss very much—but he was so unintelligent in comparison to herself that she sometimes felt embarrassed of how much she liked him. Bev's physical attractiveness gave him the early advantage over other interested young men, but time would prove that sexual attraction alone could not keep a young man in Jackie's good graces forever.

"I do think I'm in love with you when I'm with you," Jackie wrote to Bev when they had been dating for about a year and a half. "But it's awfully hard for me to stay in love with someone when I only see them every three months and when the only contact I have with them is through letters." She made an effort to see Bev in person as often as possible, but increased facetime didn't make her more confident in her love for him—in fact, it had the exact opposite effect. Jackie was interested in good-looking

boys who had an air of mischief about them—
boys who reminded her just a bit of her playboy
father, "Black Jack" Bouvier—but they could not
be stupid. That was the fatal blow for Bev; he
simply wasn't bright enough to hold Jackie's
interest permanently. Not long after leaving Miss
Porter's, Jackie let Bev down for good. "I've
always thought of being in love as being willing
to do anything for the other person—starve to
buy them bread and not mind living in Siberia
with them—and I've always thought that every
minute away from them would be hell—so
looking at it that way I guess I'm not in love with
you."

College and travel abroad

Every well-bred young woman in Jackie's social
set saw marriage as their ultimate destiny, and
Jackie was no exception. But unlike many of her
former classmates, she saw marriage, not as a

destination in itself, but as the first step towards some more interesting fate. When asked to give a quote for her Miss Porter's senior yearbook regarding her ambitions for her future life, she simply wrote, "Not to be a housewife!" She wanted to be married, certainly, but as she had once explained to Bev, she couldn't think of a worse or drearier fate than being a housewife in some small New England farming town, where the most interesting thing that was likely to happen to her was competing in bake-offs with other housewives. She was vague about precisely what kind of career she expected her future husband to propel her into, however. She did not yet know enough of the wider world to know precisely what it was that she wanted. She defined her aspirations chiefly in terms of what did *not* want to do: she did not want to be bored, she did not want to live the exact same life that every woman she knew was living, and she did not want a husband who would demand that she suppress every aspect of her personality and individuality in order to conform to the generic mold of a society matron. Her desire to avoid that fate would lead her to make some highly unconventional choices for a young woman her age over the next few years.

The summer after she graduated from Miss Porter's, Jackie entered her debutante year. She was also preparing to attend college, but this was of secondary importance to everyone, including Jackie, who was not enthused by the prospect of going to Vassar. She had wanted to attend Sarah Lawrence College, which was a fairly short drive from Manhattan, with its nightclubs and theaters and restaurants. But her father, who would be paying her tuition, wanted Jackie safely ensconced far away from temptation. He insisted on Vassar precisely because it was situated in the same sort of dull, respectable New England farming town as Miss Porter's. Jackie knew in advance that she would be terribly bored there, and determined that she would spend as little time on campus as she could get away with. She was not expected to perform brilliantly, or win academic prizes. College was seen as a safe place to stash girls who needed to pass the time while their future husbands, who were usually older than them and had already received their degrees, got started in their careers. It was normal for girls to drop out of college early once a suitable matrimonial prospect presented itself. Vassar was not a charm school in the 1940s any more than it is now, and Jackie was no intellectual lightweight. Yet when she was named "Queen Deb" at the end of her debutante season, it was seen by everyone as an accomplishment that was far more relevant to her future happiness than the degree in French she was working towards.

Jackie's debutante year—including the parties in her honor, and the wardrobe she required to attend them—was financed by her step-father, beginning with a "tea dance" for some three hundred guests hosted at one of the Auchincloss estates, called Hammersmith Farm. Accordingly, the articles about Jackie that appeared in the society pages spoke only of the generosity and prestige of her wealthy step-father; they made no mention of Jack Bouvier, who was infuriated at his erasure from the scene. Jackie was his oldest daughter, his favorite, the child who looked the most like him, and he wanted to claim some of the credit for how well she had turned out. Janet Auchincloss simply suggested that he throw his own party for Jackie if he wanted their relationship to be noticed by the papers. This was impossible, of course; any party that Jack Bouvier was capable of paying for was bound to be second rate compared to what Hugh Auchincloss had already done on Jackie's behalf. Both father and daughter would be humiliated by the inevitable comparisons.

Despite his inability to compete with Hugh Auchincloss's wealth, Jack Bouvier was the parent that Jackie felt closest to. Janet was conscious of Jackie's partiality, and she deeply resented the loyalty her daughters felt for their father. If the fate of her children had been left in Jack's hands, they would never have had the same opportunities in life, and probably would not have amounted to much—at least by Janet's standards. Jack drank too much and was too self pitying to ever reverse the decline in his fortunes. By contrast, Janet was a survivor who had done what she deemed necessary to secure her own future and advance the interests of her children. She felt that this entitled her to the greater share of Jackie's love, despite the fact that her parenting style was sometimes less than loving— one biographer describes Janet as "a drinker, a yeller, a carper, a spanker, and a slapper". Janet undoubtedly took on the lion's share of responsibility for raising Jackie and Lee, but the girls had spent weekends at Jack's apartment before her remarriage, and as is often the case in divorced families, these brief but regular visits had turned Jack into the "fun" parent. That was how Jackie thought of him even as she grew older and their visits grew less frequent. As a child, when she grew angry with her mother, Jackie would speak of wanting to go and live with Jack permanently. But this was never a possibility; both Janet and Jack knew that his Manhattan bachelor pad was no place for a young girl to grow up. Jack understood that Auchincloss's wealth and connections could help ensure his daughter the glittering future they both felt she deserved, but, quite understandably, he also resented being usurped by Auchincloss in the paternal role.

Vassar and beyond

In 1947, Jackie Bouvier, eighteen years old, became a student at Vassar College—or "that goddamn Vassar", as she referred to it. She left campus whenever the opportunity presented itself, attending parties and dances hosted by her parents' friends in New York. There, she was introduced to a preview of the life she would soon be expected to lead, the same life as every other wealthy woman she knew. Her adult responsibilities would involve catering to the needs of her husband and family; any spare time she had would be devoted to volunteer work. The parties and balls that Jackie was invited to during her deb year were usually fundraisers for the same charitable causes she would one day be expected to champion. Unofficially, of course they were also marriage markets, like the rounds of cocktail parties at her family's home in Newport.

Despite the fact that Jackie had been named Queen Deb, the real prize—engagement to the right man—had eluded her. All around her, girls she'd grown up alongside and attended school with were planning their weddings, or even anticipating the birth of their first child, but for Jackie, adulthood remained on hold. She had met with no shortage of handsome, charming, eligible marriage prospects, but having gotten a taste of the life of a society matron, she began to dread any marriage that would doom her to such an existence. She was nervous about the uncertainty of her prospects, but she remained determined to wait for something else—though she still wasn't clear in her mind what that something else might be. At last, as a junior at Vassar, she decided to look to Europe for answers. Smith College, which had close ties to Vassar, was offering students in their junior year a year-long study abroad opportunity in France, at the Sorbonne. Thrilled by the possibility of leaving Vassar behind for an entire academic year, Jackie applied to the program and received permission to join the Smith group. She was headed to France—a trip that would permanently alter the course of her life.

France

In September 1949, Jackie left the United States. Her college group headed first to Grenoble, in the French Alps, for a six-week intensive language course. The following month, they traveled to Paris, where they would spend the rest of the year at the Sorbonne, studying French history. While the Smith students boarded together in dormitories, Jackie wanted to live in an environment where French would be spoken exclusively. As a result, she became the tenant of the Comtesse de Renty, a French aristocrat who had been an active part of the Resistance, and whose husband had died in a concentration camp. Jackie had been to Europe once before, but the experience had left her dissatisfied. She had traveled as part of a small, highly chaperoned group of debutantes undertaking a sort of demi-Grand Tour, but the girls had been so closely supervised, their schedule of visits and tours so rigid, that Jackie felt she had not gained much experience of what any of the countries she'd visited were really like. In Paris, however, she was only lightly chaperoned, and she was largely independent for the first time in her life.

Jackie attended university classes by day, and toured galleries and historic landmarks in the afternoons. In the evenings, she was squired about Paris by the kind of men whose existence she had intuited, but had never actually met prior to leaving home—writers, aristocrats, ambassadors, politicians, all of whom seemed far more sophisticated, cultured, and open-minded than the men she knew at home. More importantly, perhaps, Jackie gained the sense that the men she dated in France were not intimidated or repelled by a woman who possessed intelligence and opinions of her own. The time Jackie spent in Paris gave her a glimpse of a larger world. She was still vague about what, precisely, she wanted from life, apart from "not to be a housewife", but she was starting to gain a better understanding of her own ambitions. Ideally, her future life would look more like the independent existence she had led in Paris than the constrained course of her life at home.

Jackie returned to the United States reluctantly in the summer of 1950, and from that point forward, her career began to diverge sharply from the path trodden by her female forebears and peers. Compared to other girls of her age and class, she was lagging behind. This was especially evident now that her younger sister Lee was eighteen. Lee had grown up in Jackie's shadow, but she had not remained there. Like her sister, she too was crowned Queen Deb; unlike Jackie, she was considered more approachable, more fashionable, and prettier. Comparisons were inevitably made between the two girls, and Jackie again began to feel nervous that she was endangering her prospects.

Rather than competing with Lee by confining herself to the same life of charitable balls and cocktails parties she had known before her year abroad, Jackie decided to transfer from Vassar to George Washington University in Virginia, where she majored in French. She had not wanted to leave France at all, so when she spied an opportunity to return in October of her first semester, she eagerly seized it. She entered and won the Vogue Prix de Paris contest, open only to young women who were college seniors. The top prize was six months working as a junior editor at Vogue's New York office, followed by six months working in the magazine's Paris office. "As to physical appearance," she wrote, as part of her application, "I am tall, 5'7", with brown hair, a square face and eyes so unfortunately far apart that it takes three weeks to have a pair of glasses made with a bridge wide enough to fit over my nose." She also wrote an essay about the three historical figures she would have liked to have met personally: the French poet Charles Baudelaire, the Irish playwright Oscar Wilde, and the Russian art critic Sergei Diaghilev.

Jackie's winning the contest gave her something to look forward to in the autumn following her graduation from George Washington—and her step-father gave her something to look forward to over the summer as well. To celebrate Jackie's graduation from college and Lee's graduation from Miss Porter's, Hugh Auchincloss agreed to send both girls to Europe for a few months. They were due to set sail in June. Before Jackie left Washington, however, she attended a dinner party hosted by a former boyfriend, Charles Bartlett, and his wife Martha. The purpose of the dinner party was to set her up with a nice young man the couple were friends with: a World War II veteran and junior Congressman by the name of Jack Kennedy.

Unbeknownst to the Bartletts, Jackie had met Jack Kennedy once already, by chance, on a train ride from Washington to New York. It was her debutante year, and she was still at Vassar;

Kennedy had tried to flirt with her, but she had rebuffed him. He met with a similar lack of success during the Bartlett's dinner party. As the guests were leaving, Kennedy asked Jackie whether she'd like to go somewhere and have a drink. But Jackie had discovered that another male friend of hers had been driving past the Bartlett house and recognized her car parked on the street. He'd hidden in the back seat to surprise her, and Jackie, amused by the prank, chose to leave with him instead of the Congressman. Kennedy took the rejection in good grace—he never suffered from a lack of female companionship, and had asked her out mostly to please the Bartletts, who had taken so much trouble to set them up. In any case, Jackie was due to leave Washington soon for a year in New York and Paris. Their paths were unlikely to cross again for some time, if at all.

Jackie's anticipated year as a junior editor at Vogue never came to fruition, however. Her very first day on the job, she met with managing editor Carol Phillips, who would go on to found the beauty brand Clinique. Phillips seemed to home in on Jackie's insecurity regarding the fact that she was still unmarried at the age of 22, which made her practically an old maid amongst the girls of her social set. Without firing her outright, Phillips hinted strongly that Jackie should return to Washington, where her marital prospects would be better: "That's where all the boys are," she told her. Whether Jackie was genuinely ambivalent about her new job or merely intimidated by Phillips' discouragement, she chose not to return to Vogue after her first day. Instead, she returned to Washington, to reassess the marriage market there—and to look for a job.

Chapter Two: Career Ambitions

A new job

In Washington, Jackie continued to live at Merrywood, the Auchincloss mansion where she had resided with her family while she was finishing college. There, she applied for a number of different jobs, including a position at the CIA. In the end, however, Hugh Auchincloss arranged for Jackie to go to work for the Washington *Times-Herald*, where the managing editor had an eccentric habit of hiring young unmarried girls for cheap labor and fresh perspectives.

By this time, Jackie had determined that she wanted a career in journalism—or so she insisted to editor Frank Waldrop, who was initially reluctant to hire her, on the basis that she was likely to waste his time by getting married and quitting just as he'd finished training her. Jackie assured him that this wasn't the case, and that she didn't view the job at the newspaper merely as a way of passing the time until she found a husband. Waldrop told her to go home to her parents for the Christmas holidays and to show up for work in the New Year—and not to come to him in January simply to announce that she was engaged. Jackie promised that she would do no such thing.

By January of 1952, however, Jackie *was* engaged—to a young man named John G.W. Husted, Jr. Their courtship had begun suddenly and progressed rapidly, and that was what had chiefly recommended it to Jackie. She had always cherished a romantic, poetic notion that true love happened to people all at once, bursting in on their dull lives like a miracle. Husted, 24, had fallen in love with Jackie practically at first sight, perceiving her as a shy, naïve creature, like "a deer that has just come out of the woods and beheld its first human being". The swiftness of his feelings for her practically guaranteed that Jackie would return them, at least at first. Things began to go wrong, however, as soon as she was introduced to Husted's mother. Helen Husted had, like Jackie, been a Miss Porter's student, then a successful debutante who married a banker before she was twenty and had afterwards settled down to a typical career of volunteer work and looking after her husband and family. Visiting with her, Jackie realized that Husted, his family, and everyone else she knew would expect her to live the exact same life his mother had led—no variations, no surprises. A sense of oppression settled over her as the older woman showed her family photo albums, and Jackie grew uncharacteristically snappish. The visit was not a success.

Husted seemed not to notice that Jackie was having doubts about their future together. Shortly after introducing her to his mother, he asked Jackie to marry him, presenting her with the same engagement ring that his mother had once worn. Despite her misgivings, Jackie accepted Husted's proposal, and when the Christmas holidays were over, she faced Frank Waldrop to tell him, with serious embarrassment, that she was, after all, engaged. Waldrop's reaction surprised her. Rather than railing at her, he simply asked her how long she had known her fiancé. When she told him that they'd only known each other for a month, Waldrop seemed relieved. "Hell, there's nothing to that," he told her. "Get to work."

Jackie was to serve as Waldrop's secretary-receptionist. According to him, her duties would consist primarily of saying "Thank you very much for calling" about a hundred times a day, and converting Waldrop's shouts of "Tell him to go to hell!" into politely worded correspondence. Curiously, Jackie had been preceded in her position as secretary-receptionist at the *Times-*

Herald by Kathleen "Kick" Kennedy, the sister of the man the Bartletts had unsuccessfully attempted to set her up with the previous year.

During Kathleen Kennedy's tenure at the *Times-Herald,* she had dated a features reporter named Jack White. White was wildly in love with Kathleen, but the relationship had foundered because he could not convince her to sleep with him—Kathleen cherished strict Catholic principles prohibiting sex outside of marriage. After their relationship dissolved, Kathleen had gone on to marry a British aristocrat whom she'd met during her father's tenure as the American ambassador to the Court of St. James. Kathleen was widowed when her husband was killed in action during the war; a few years later, in 1948, Kathleen herself was killed in a plane crash.

White had not seen Kathleen for several years by the time of her death, but he was devastated by her loss all the same. Now forty years old, an ex-Marine working for the State Department, White continued to spend a good deal of time hanging around the *Times-Herald,* in an effort to relive the best years of his youth. This involved flirting with the pretty young women who had succeeded to Kathleen Kennedy's position as Waldorp's secretary. When White heard through the grapevine that Waldorp had recently hired a 22-year old former Queen Deb named Jackie Bouvier, he made a point of visiting his old friend for the expression purpose of finagling an introduction to her. That introduction would serve as the great turning point of Jackie's life.

Jackie Bouvier, Inquiring Photographer

White had been convinced that Kathleen Kennedy was a journalistic prodigy, wasted on secretarial work; he had been her mentor in journalism as well as her would-be lover. He had not known Jackie Bouvier for long before he decided that she was cut from the same cloth as Kathleen. At White's insistence, Waldorp gave Jackie a new job—for $42.50 a week, she would be an "inquiring photographer", wandering scenic parts of Washington with a camera. Her job was to approach people, ask their opinions on some given subject, then take their picture. It was light journalism at best, but it was a position far better suited to Jackie's natural curiosity and adventurousness than answering phones and writing correspondence.

White was deeply taken with Jackie, but for once in his life—he was a notorious womanizer—he kept the relationship on strictly platonic ground. He convinced Waldorp to give her more serious assignments for the newspaper, and in the mean time he started inviting her to gatherings at "the cave", which was his name for his apartment in the basement of his sister's house. White's gatherings were generally attended by other male journalists, including men who had reported from overseas during the war. Spending time in their company reminded Jackie of the time she'd spent in Paris, being escorted around the city by men whose more varied experience of life made the men she knew back home seem uncultured, narrow-minded, and boring.

It was John Husted's misfortune that he was formed in the same mold as every other man Jackie had ever dated—the only thing that had set him apart was his romantic nature, which had helped convince her that she was deeply in love with him. But no amount of romance would save her from a life of upper class domestic drudgery if she married him. Husted's standing with Jackie was also damaged by the fact that he considered her work for the *Times-Herald* in the light of an amusing pastime, a hobby to keep her busy until their wedding. White, by contrast, was helping Jackie grow into her role as a journalist by encouraging her to "have fun and take chances". He nurtured her confidence in her abilities, while Husted, who came down from New York every weekend to visit her and often accompanied her while she made the rounds of Washington with her camera, declared that her job was "insipid". Soon, it scarcely mattered that Jackie's relationship with White was platonic. If anything, he was more of a threat to Husted *because* he wasn't trying to steal Jackie away from him. If White had appeared in the light of an interested suitor, Jackie would have felt duty-bound to be reserved and stand-offish with him. Instead, he was helping her to become the person she wanted to be—and that person could not see herself conforming to the pattern of life that would be expected of her as Husted's wife.

Yet the death knell for Jackie's engagement to Husted did not begin to ring until, during one of White's gatherings, she came face to face with Jack Kennedy for the third time. White and Kennedy had mutually loathed one another while Kathleen Kennedy was alive, but after her death, the two men had found themselves drawn together by their mutual loss. Jack and Kathleen had been as close as twins, after all; by spending time with Kennedy, White sometimes remembered how it had felt to be close to his sister. They also had in common the hobby of sleeping with as many women as they possibly could, though White did not mention this to Jackie, at first.

When White's sister introduced Jackie to Kennedy, she was under the impression that it was their first meeting. In some ways, it was not dissimilar to a first encounter. By now, Jackie knew all about Kathleen's death and Kennedy's tragic loss, and about his journalistic work—in 1945, Kennedy had made headlines by calling the British general election for the Labour Party, even though Winston Churchill, a Tory, was considered unbeatable. He had known suffering, and he had a keen mind. Possession of this knowledge made Jackie look at Kennedy, who had previously struck her as an overgrown frat boy, with new eyes. Kennedy, similarly, was newly intrigued by Jackie. The fact that she had forsaken the expected career of a former Queen Deb to pursue journalism and live an independent life made her far more interesting to him than before. He'd flirted with her in a casual way during their first two meetings, but now, suddenly, he was blasting all his considerable charm for her benefit. Yet much to White's amusement, Jackie continued to rebuff Kennedy. She was still engaged to another man, after all, and even if she was having doubts about her relationship with Husted, it would be against her principles to encourage Kennedy's attentions while she still wore his ring.

Kennedy, like White a hardened womanizer who enjoyed nothing more than "the chase", found that Jackie's aloofness only made her more attractive to him, and he gradually began to wear down her resistance. Before long, Kennedy and Jackie were seen together in Washington so often that Jackie felt the need to write to John Husted and urge him to ignore any gossip he might hear about their friendship.

However, in March of 1952, only three months after she had taken the job at the *Times-Herald,* Jackie finally came to the conclusion that she could not marry him. Many factors influenced her decision: Husted's refusal to take her career seriously, the stultifying life that marriage to him would entail, the glimpse of a broader world that was afforded to her by her association with White, as well as her budding relationship with Kennedy. All these things combined to convince her that she must end the engagement. Husted, none the wiser, traveled from New York to Washington for one final weekend visit. When he boarded the train on Sunday afternoon, Jackie dropped his mother's engagement ring into his pocket. The meaning of such a gesture was unmistakable.

To spare Husted's feelings, Jackie told him that she had changed her mind because her mother opposed their marriage, on the grounds that his family was not wealthy enough, and he himself did not earn a large enough salary, to keep her in the style she was accustomed to as Hugh Auchincloss's step-daughter. This was true, as far as it went, but it would not have deterred Jackie from marrying him if she had been willing to undertake the lifestyle that marriage to him represented.

Jack and Jackie

Jack Kennedy was twelve years Jackie Bouvier's senior, and while the age gap was not considered an obstacle to their marriage, it made a considerable difference in their maturity levels. One wonders whether Jackie would have been willing to marry him if she had been a little older, or had possessed a better understanding of powerful men and the behavior they expected their wives to let them get away with.

In 1952, Jack Kennedy's speech, behavior, appearance, and manner of dress all made him appear younger than he was, more like the fraternity boy Jackie had seen at their first two meetings than a serious politician serving as a member of Congress. There was certainly nothing in his career so far to suggest that he was a future president in the making. Kennedy was not well-respected in Washington. He was regarded, with some justification, as a playboy whose wealthy father had essentially purchased his seat in the House of Representatives. This perception of him had arisen due partly to the fact that Kennedy loudly broadcasted the notion that he had never wanted to enter politics in the first place. That, after all, was the career which his father, Joseph Kennedy, had always envisioned for his older brother, Joe Jr.

The idea that Jack Kennedy never would have pursued politics if it had not been for Joe Jr.'s death is an ingrained aspect of his legend, but it couldn't be further from the truth. Kennedy was highly motivated to enter politics, and deeply ambitious from the time he was a young man. While serving as ambassador to England, Joseph Kennedy had told a number of people that he expected his oldest son to become the first Irish-Catholic president of the United States. These plans had changed after his second son's first book, *Why England Slept*, was published. Joseph had encouraged Joe Jr. to write about his time in England as a means of generating publicity for his future political career. But Joe Jr. was no scholar, and his "second-rate" essays and letters had been received with polite rejections from various magazines. There was simply no depth to his opinions. His brother Jack, however, possessed what he did not—the historical perspectives and knowledge of current events necessary to produce an informed analysis of international politics leading up to the war.

Joe Jr. was a tall, handsome, robust youth who had been more interested in throwing a football around as a child than in reading. His father, though unstinting in his affection towards Jack, made no secret of his belief that Jack's physical frailty made him an unsuitable vehicle for his ambitions. But Jack's many childhood illnesses had conferred a hidden advantage. He was often confined to bed for weeks with nothing to do but read, and think about what he'd read. He knew that he possessed greater political acumen than his older brother, but he had never been able to persuade his father, who could not see past Joe Jr.'s outward appearance of superiority. *Why England Slept* was written out of Jack's desire to prove to Joseph, once and for all, that it was he, not Joe Jr., who possessed the qualities necessary for leadership. It was, after all, exactly the kind of book Joseph had wanted and expected Joe Jr. to be able to write. It had not even occurred to him to challenge Jack to make his own literary effort. Yet it took Jack only six months to write his astute appraisal of England's reluctance during the early 1930s to check Hitler's domination of eastern Europe. As a ploy to win his father's esteem, it was an unqualified success.

After *Why England Slept* was published to critical acclaim and best-seller status, Joseph transferred his political ambitions onto Jack's shoulders almost overnight. Physically, Jack would always be inferior to Joe Jr.—he had been diagnosed with Addison's disease, a deficiency of the adrenal glands which renders sufferers unusually susceptible to infections. He was also plagued by a weak back, a condition which was probably worsened by the spinal injury he had sustained during the war. But none of that mattered to Joseph Kennedy anymore. He had crowned Jack as his heir long before Joe Jr. was killed in action. The idea that Jack Kennedy had been forced by his brother's tragic death to take up his banner was nothing more than an extremely effective fabrication that served as the rhetorical cornerstone of his campaign speeches. He wanted very much to be in Washington, and had worked extremely hard to get there.

But Kennedy's effectiveness on the campaign trail did not translate to great deeds on the floor of Congress, any more than his intellectual depth had conferred emotional maturity in his sexual relationships. Years of scrapping unsuccessfully with his older brother for their father's attention had shaped him into a figure not unlike Shakespeare's Prince Hal. It suited him to play the part of a slacker, quietly biding his time until he was ready to make a decisive move, and the time for such a move had not yet arrived, though it was fast approaching. In early 1952, right around the time that Kennedy was becoming re-acquainted with Jackie Bouvier, his father was deciding that he should challenge incumbent Republican senator Henry Cabot Lodge in the November election of that year. There was just one problem: Kennedy's image in Washington would have to undergo serious rehabilitation if he was to have any chance of advancing to a higher office. He had been socially rejected by a prominent political host in Washington after he was heard to complain that there were never enough pretty girls at his dinner parties.

Kennedy would have to change the way he was perceived if anyone was going to take him seriously as a prospective senator. The simplest, most effective way for him to do this was by marrying and starting a family. Yet, this was also a problem, in that Kennedy had absolutely no desire to marry.

After meeting her at White's gatherings, Kennedy had pursued Jackie with great enthusiasm. She was interesting, attractive, and most importantly, engaged to another man. Chasing after unavailable women was Kennedy's favorite recreational activity; married women, and women who were engaged, could be counted on to provide him with amusement, without threatening him by angling for a proposal. He seemed to feel that the bane of his existence was the kind of woman who "won't leave me alone". In this, he displayed a specific weakness found in many wealthy, powerful men who have been raised to believe that they must marry strategically, for the good of their families. Charles, Prince of Wales, notoriously informed his young wife Diana that his previous girlfriends had almost all been married women, because they were "safe".

Jackie, by comparison, had only resisted Kennedy's advances because she did not want to hurt John Husted's feelings. She was young, sincere, and had been brought up to regard marriage as the most serious and important decision of her life, and it was not in her nature to play the kind of sexual games that Kennedy delighted in. She had returned Husted's ring in large part because she had decided that Kennedy, who seemed to want her very much, was the man for her. The end of her engagement was the outward sign of her readiness to be courted seriously.

Both Jackie and Kennedy had a duty to marry someone, and soon—Jackie, because that was her destiny as a woman, and Kennedy, to serve his career. But Jackie, who had been required to think seriously about what she required in a husband since she was sixteen, knew by now what she wanted in a husband. She wanted a man who was both intelligent and attractive, who was wealthy, and who could provide her with a more interesting life than that of a typical society matron. Jack Kennedy could offer her all of these things. She was not unaware that he kept company with numerous other women—Jack White, who probably knew more about Kennedy's sexual exploits than anyone else, had made a point of enlightening her—but Jackie's feeling was that a little wildness in a husband was no bad thing, and that for the most part she could probably keep him in line. Her willingness to overlook his promiscuity can be explained in part by youthful idealism and in part by the fact that she had already learned to love and accept another notorious womanizer—her father. As biographer Barbara Leaming writes,

"Even those personal qualities that some women might regard as deal breakers only made Jack the more attractive to Jackie. She thought him excitingly unconventional and unpredictable, full of angles and surprises, in the way that her father had been. And if, like Black Jack Bouvier, Jack Kennedy was also a little

dangerous, so much the better; at least he was
not bland and boring like the fellow she had
almost married. At the same time, it struck
certain of Kennedy's friends that Jackie thought
she could succeed with him where her mother
had failed with Black Jack; that drawn as she was
to the bad boy in Kennedy, she believed she was
the one to change him."

In other words, Kennedy possessed all the
attributes she required in a husband, with the
added bonus that he evoked the same sexual
charisma she associated with Jack Bouvier.
Kennedy also had a laundry list of attributes he
required in a wife, and Jackie, as it happened,
possessed all of them. But though he liked her,
he did not love her, and more importantly, he
didn't want to marry anyone, however suitable
they might be. It was Joseph Kennedy who had
decided that Jack required a wife, and that
Jackie Bouvier was the right woman for him. She
was suitable in Joseph's eyes because she was

Roman Catholic—the Kennedys were devout and would not marry outside the Church—but thanks to her mother's second marriage, she also possessed strong family ties to the conservative world of upper class Wasp society. Her aristocratic connections were exactly what the upstart Kennedys, with their new money and their Boston Irish background, lacked. Yet just as Jackie decided to end her engagement with John Husted and allow Kennedy to court her in good faith, it became Kennedy's turn to grow aloof. Never mind that he liked her, that she could help his career, or that his father was keen on her. As soon as she became available, as soon as marriage was on the table, he grew cold.

The Senator's wife

The marriage of Jackie Bouvier to Jack Kennedy depended, ultimately, on whether or not Kennedy defeated Henry Cabot Lodge and gained his seat in the Senate. It can only be guessed whether Jackie was fully conscious of this, but either way, she took an avid interest in the progress of his campaign. While serving as a naval officer in World War II, Kennedy's patrol boat had come under attack from the Japanese, and Kennedy had sustained serious injuries to his back when he was thrown against the prow of the ship. Doctors were divided as to whether this, or congenital weakness of the spine, was to blame for the fact that he was often in excruciating pain, but the war injury made for a better story on the campaign trail. The pain was so debilitating during the 1952 campaign that Kennedy was usually forced to walk on crutches between stops. Jackie was deeply moved by the contrast between the agonized Kennedy struggling to cross a room, and the energized, magnetic Kennedy who mounted podiums and delivered speeches to thunderous applause.

When Kennedy won the election over Lodge in November of 1952, he invited Jackie to accompany him as his date to president-elect Dwight Eisenhower's inaugural ball. But if Jackie expected a rapid engagement to follow after Kennedy's victory, she was disappointed. Kennedy continued dating other women for a few months, including the actress Aubrey Hepburn, who had something of Jackie's look—androgynous, dark haired, with wide eyes. During the campaign, Jackie had told herself that it was natural for Kennedy to be too busy to pay much attention to her. But with the campaign over, and with two months to go before he would be sworn into his Senate seat, she could no longer deceive herself. He simply wasn't the devoted suitor she had believed him to be. Yet despite being offended by his vacillation, she continued to act the part of a loving girlfriend, sometimes using her French language skills to assist him in his work. She had been brought up to approach the acquisition of the right husband in much the same light that

Kennedy approached his political career. If Kennedy was getting cold feet, it was her job to maneuver him skillfully into warmer climes. When Kennedy returned to Washington for the opening of the Senate, Jackie set about proving her devotion to him by featuring him in her "Inquiring Camera Girl" column, dialing up the seriousness of the questions she normally asked her interviewees to reflect the seriousness of his job. While Congress was debating whether to send troops to Indochina (French Vietnam), Jackie translated French books and document to help with his research.

Most of Jackie's friends and family, including her mother and Jack White, thought that her efforts were more likely to drive Kennedy further away than reel him in. Her mother wasn't sure Kennedy had ever meant to marry her, though she herself desperately wanted the marriage to take place—the Kennedys were incredibly wealthy, and Jackie would at last be on equal footing with the Auchincloss clan. Jack White also thought it was unlikely that Kennedy would ever marry her, but unlike Jackie's mother, he urged her to turn him down even if he did propose. Well acquainted as he was with Kennedy's promiscuous exploits, he knew Jackie would probably be unhappy as his wife. In an act of what turned out to be wishful thinking, White bet Jackie a dollar that the wedding would never take place.

Jack White was sitting in the back pew of St. Mary's Roman Catholic Church in Newport, Rhode Island, on the day that Jackie Bouvier became Jackie Kennedy. He was waving a dollar bill in the air, to the bafflement of those seated around him, but Jackie, who was walking back down the aisle on her husband's arm after saying her vows, burst into laughter when she saw him. It was one of few carefree moments that Jackie enjoyed on her wedding day. Getting to the altar had been grueling enough, and the wedding itself was a garish, glaringly public ordeal. But that had been true of every occasion the couple had celebrated together since Jackie had accepted Kennedy's proposal. They had not been engaged long before Jackie began to realize that the man of her dreams was more dream than substance.

In the end, Kennedy had proposed to Jackie, not as a result of the painstaking effort she had put into their relationship, but because her mother, an experienced manipulator of powerful men, had wielded her own expertise. Both she and Black Jack Bouvier had insisted that if Jackie wanted Kennedy to propose to her, she would have to return to playing hard to get. She must be aloof and unavailable, they insisted, though this ran entirely contrary to the instincts of a young woman sincerely in love. Janet had finally suggested that Jackie travel to England to cover the coronation of Elizabeth II for the Washington *Times-Herald*. In her opinion, Jackie needed to prove to Kennedy that she had a complicated and interesting life of her own, and that if he continued to neglect her, she was perfectly capable of going back to it and forgetting all about him. If Frank Waldorp wasn't willing to cover the cost of the trip, Janet told her, she would be happy the buy the plane tickets herself. Jackie balked at first, but eventually allowed herself to be persuaded. Janet's maneuver paid off: Kennedy proposed to Jackie by telegram while she was still in England, and met her as she was getting off the plane upon her return home.

Jackie was delighted. Janet was delighted. But no one was more delighted than Joseph Kennedy. He promptly invited Jackie to come and meet the entire Kennedy clan at their house in Hyannis Port. Jackie had anticipated a quiet, intimate visit with her future in-laws, but Joseph had a different purpose in mind. Photographers and reporters from *Life* magazine had also been invited to the house for the purpose of showcasing the handsome young senator from Massachusetts as he courted his newly affianced wife. Unbeknownst to Jackie, her newly affianced husband was due to take a vacation to the south of France immediately after her visit, a vacation which Joseph Kennedy knew would involve his son coaxing as many girls into his bed as he possibly could. As a precaution against scandal, Joseph wrote to his son's old Harvard roommate, Torby Macdonald, asking him to do everything he could to keep Kennedy's dalliances discreet. This would involve such chores as flirting with women on Kennedy's behalf and running interference with any reporters who might chance to be in the area. "As I told you, I am hoping that he will take a rest and not jump about from place to place, and be especially mindful of whom he sees," Joseph wrote to Macdonald. It was crucial to all of Joseph Kennedy's plans that his son's marriage to Jackie Bouvier go ahead without a hitch—and if Kennedy were photographed in an intimate embrace with another woman, a hitch would most certainly arise.

Throughout their engagement, Jackie and Kennedy spent hardly any time alone together— another thing the couple had in common with the Prince and Princess of Wales. Whenever Jackie came to Hyannis Port, she was surrounded at all times by Kennedy family members. More strangely, whenever Kennedy visited Jackie at Hammersmith Farm, Torby Macdonald accompanied him, and often spent more time talking to Jackie than Kennedy did. Jackie found this bewildering, but she was prepared to make any number of allowances for Kennedy, who, she had often been advised, was older than her and thus set in his ways. His ways, apparently, included surrounding himself at all times with old school friends, college chums, and acquaintances from his London days, many of whom were overawed by Kennedy's status and wealth and functioned as sycophants to the family's interests.

Joseph Kennedy did his best to ensure that his son's eccentric behavior wouldn't give Jackie a case of cold feet by cultivating her himself. His affection for her was genuine—she reminded him, as she had reminded Jack White, and possibly Jack Kennedy, of his daughter Kathleen, the only one of his daughters he'd felt he could really talk to. And Jackie was equally enraptured by her new father in law, despite the fact that he crassly and unapologetically put her relationship with his son on display to reporters at every opportunity, as part of his general program to rehabilitate Kennedy's political image. Joseph tended to compartmentalize his feelings for people from his assessment of them as political assets—a fact which came as a rude surprise to Jackie when she overheard Joseph discussing her in rather cold terms with her new husband. In most respects, Joseph Kennedy displayed more warmth and consideration for Jackie's feelings than Jack did. But his affection for her did not prevent him from trampling on the wishes of both Jackie and her family when it came to planning the wedding.

Janet, Hugh Auchincloss, and Jackie all wanted a simple, quiet ceremony at St. Mary's. Joseph insisted on turning the wedding into the same media-courting spectacle as Jackie's first visit to Hyannis Port, only more so. The wedding ceremony was an occasion for deeply mixed feelings on Jackie's part. Not only was she uncomfortable with being put on display, but her father had not shown up to walk her down the aisle. She was escorted by Hugh Auchincloss instead. Joseph Kennedy told reporters that Jack Bouvier had come down with a severe case of the flu. In reality, he had gotten extremely drunk the night before to cope with the ordeal of spending hours in a church with both the Kennedys and the Auchincloss clan; the time of the wedding had come and gone while he was passed out in bed.

Yet, at the end of the ceremony, Jack White was waiting with his one dollar bill to make Jackie laugh. And when all was said and done, Jackie was now the wife of the man she thought she had been waiting for her whole life. For a short time—just about two weeks—she was destined to be simply, spectacularly happy. Joseph Kennedy had arranged a magnificent surprise for their honeymoon trip to Acapulco. She'd mentioned to him, in passing, that she had once glimpsed a beautiful house in Mexico that had struck her as the ideal honeymoon getaway. Joseph had managed to track down the house and its owner (a former president of Mexico) and retain it, along with the services of three maids, for as long as Senator Kennedy and his new bride should wish to stay there. The two weeks that Jack and Jackie spent in the pink-tiled house in Acapulco was the first significant period of time they had ever spent alone in each other's company. Kennedy's health, rarely robust, was good for the duration of the honeymoon, and Jackie derived a great deal of amusement from the fact that her husband had to ask her to translate his instructions to the servants whenever he needed anything.

Then, their time in Mexico came to an end, and they flew to Los Angeles for the second leg of their honeymoon. To Jackie's dismay, almost as soon as they arrived, Kennedy invited another couple to join them, putting an end to their privacy. Then he suggested that Jackie fly back to Hyannis Port alone while he remained in California a little longer. Jackie was stunned by the request, and refused to leave without him. At that point in their marriage, she did not yet realize that Kennedy had no intention of leaving his promiscuous ways behind at the altar, and that his request for time alone in California was almost certainly due to the fact that he was hoping to arrange a few quick dalliances to relieve the tedium of less than a month of marital fidelity. But she would learn quickly. "It's not important what you really are," Joseph Kennedy often told his sons. "The only important thing is what people think you are." Over the course of the next ten years, the length of her marriage to Jack Kennedy, Jackie would be forced to learn how to play things Joseph's way.

Chapter Three: A Decade of Marriage

Profiles in Courage

By October of 1954, when the Kennedys had been married for a little over two years, Jack Kennedy was facing the greatest health crisis of a lifetime that had been littered with such crises. Jack sometimes suffered excruciating pain due to his weak back, but what had once been a misery was now simply unendurable. He consulted with surgeons, who proposed a double spinal fusion. There was just one catch: Kennedy's Addison's disease made him a poor candidate for any kind of surgery, let alone a lengthy, risky procedure such as the one the surgeons were proposing. Jack's endocrinologist, Elmer Bartels, who had been treating him for years and made a point of being available to his patients at any inconvenient hour of the day or night, flew to the hospital on the day of the surgery for the express purpose of trying to talk Jack out of having the procedure.

But Kennedy had been living with illness for so long that it had turned him into an inveterate risk taker. He'd had his first brush with death during a bout of scarlet fever when he was only two years old, and in London, the doctors who had diagnosed him with Addison's disease told him that he was unlikely to live out the rest of the year. Elmer Bartels dismissed this prognosis and told Kennedy that so long as he was consistent about taking his medication—which he sometimes failed to do—and avoided undue trauma, there was no reason he should not live a normal lifespan. But now that Kennedy's back pain was so severe as to make it almost impossible for him to stand on the floor of the Senate to deliver a speech, subjecting himself to surgical trauma appeared to be his only option. His doctors, family, and friends all tried to talk him out of the procedure, but Jack's mind was made up. "I don't care," Jackie overheard him saying to his father. "I can't go on like this."

The three-hour surgery very nearly lived up to Elmer Bartels' direst prognostications. Kennedy developed a urinary tract infection only a few hours after he was wheeled out of the operating room. He lapsed into a coma, and his doctors advised his family that he probably would not live through the night. A priest was called, and last rites were administered. Jackie sat by his bedside—praying, she later claimed, for the first time in her life. Even when Kennedy recovered from the coma, he remained extremely weak. The surgeons had inserted a metal disc into his spine in hopes of stabilizing it, but the presence of the disc left him in even worse pain than he had been in before the operation. Worse, the eight-inch long surgical scar wasn't healing—it oozed and gave off a bad smell, and the dressings had to be changed several times a day. Worse still was the depression that Kennedy suffered during the long weeks that followed, weeks of not being able to stand, walk, sit up straight, or even lie on his back. Nothing seemed to help, not even being transferred to the Kennedy house in Palm Beach, the first floor of which had been turned into a convalescent's retreat, complete with hospital bed. The negative psychological impact of the failed surgery was so devastating that members of his family, including Joseph Kennedy, feared that he was ruined—for politics, for marriage, for any kind of decent life.

After doctors determined that Kennedy's surgical scar had become infected, he was returned to the hospital for a second surgery, during which the metal disc in his spine was removed. The endocrinologist who had consulted on his case— not Elmer Bartels—admitted that he had been of the opinion that the surgery should not proceed, but had withheld his objections out of deference to the orthopedic surgeon. Now that it was apparent that a spinal fusion would never be successful, he recommended that Kennedy consult Dr. Janet Travell, a pain specialist who would treat Kennedy's back pain with frequent injections of procaine, a drug similar to lidocaine and Novocain. Travell's treatments did not eliminate the pain, but they reduced it to a level that Kennedy considered manageable. Upon his return to Washington, he declared to reporters that he was almost entirely recovered—and he proceeded to prove it by walking up the steps of the Capitol building unaided. Afterwards, he was in agony, but he was satisfied that he had proved his point.

Throughout Kennedy's long convalescence, three things had tethered him to life. The first was Jackie's constant care and nursing. Jack had been severely ill on so many occasions that he had made up his mind, after receiving his Addison's diagnosis, that he probably would not live past middle age. The fact that he held such a conviction probably explains a great deal about his stubbornness, his relentless drive, and his willingness to take risks. Jackie, by contrast, had never before had to cope with serious illness, either in herself or in a loved one. She had certainly never before sat next to a family member's bed while they hovered between life and death. Not everyone is capable of rising to the occasion during such a crisis, but Jackie put aside her shock and grief and devoted herself to her husband's care. Jack's medical problems were a closely guarded secret—his political image was founded, in part, on the fact that he was supposed to represent the new young post-war generation of politicians. Partly because of this, and partly because Joseph Kennedy was frightened of scaring Jackie off, she had received only the faintest hints, prior to their marriage, of the extent of Jack's health issues. The crisis which had led to the surgery came as no surprise to his family, but it came as a considerable shock to Jackie, who was forced to accept the possibility, even the likelihood, that she would become a widow a mere two years into her marriage. Many a young wife in her situation might have felt some justifiable resentment towards her husband's family for their lack of candor, but Jackie's only concern was to help Jack get back on his feet.

Jackie was also of considerable help to Kennedy when it came to other matters important to his recovery. At the very point when it seemed that depression might well be the most critical threat to his health, he seemed to remember the comfort that books and reading had brought him when he was ill as a child. He was no longer capable of holding a book, or a pen, but during the endless weeks he had spent lying immobile on his stomach, he had put together the concept for the book that would eventually become *Profiles in Courage*, which examined the question of whether politicians had a moral duty to put the interests of their country and constituency first, even when doing so would jeopardize their hold on power. Kennedy was not a strong prose stylist, and even when he was strong enough to hold a pen he depended on ghostwriters to help him put his concepts into words. But while he was bed-bound, he also required someone to acquire books, read aloud to him, take dictation, and hire research assistants—and this, in addition to supervising his medical care, became Jackie's job.

The third key to Kennedy's physical and mental recovery from the surgery that had nearly claimed his life was his frantic attempts to arrange a romantic rendezvous with a young Swedish woman named Gunilla von Post, whom he had met during his trip to the south of France just after he became engaged to Jackie. Whenever Jackie was not in the room, he was scrawling short letters and placing international phone calls, trying to convince Gunilla to meet him in the summer, by which point he was convinced he would have recovered the athleticism that would be necessary for such an encounter. Once Kennedy had finished work on the book and had returned to Washington to resume the Senate seat he had been forced to leave vacant for months, he immediately began devising a plan that would enable him to act on the fantasy which had sustained him for so long. The first prong of this plan involved sending Jackie, with her sister Lee, to England for several months. He painted this trip to Jackie as a special gift, given out of gratitude for her strength and devotion during his illness, and to help her recuperate from the effects of the long strain she'd been under. He would be sending her to stay with friends and relatives of his sister Kathleen's husband, Billy Hartington—English aristocrats who had come to regard Kick and her brother as members of the family. Once the Congressional recess began, Kennedy assured Jackie, they would meet in Antibes, for a proper vacation together.

Jackie had, in truth, performed above and beyond the call of duty during her husband's long ordeal, and she was genuinely eager to do as he suggested and get away from it all for a few months. She appreciated what she perceived to be a self-sacrificing gesture of gratitude on his part, and confessed herself eager to meet the English friends of whom Jack spoke so often, who had been such an important part of his life before the war. The fact that Jack's supposed grateful gesture was also a ruse intended to get her out of the way so that he could spend a week in the bed of another woman is painful to contemplate. But on this occasion, his faithlessness received the reward it deserved: when the long-awaited trip to Sweden actually transpired, it quickly dissolved into farce, when his mistress, Gunilla von Post, greeted him surrounded by her large extended family, including her parents, and her cousin Eric von Post, who was the Swedish ambassador to Poland. Rather than a week of private, secret trysts with Gunilla, he found himself surrounded by people who all seemed to know perfectly well that he was a married American senator with presidential ambitions. The icing on the cake, at least for anyone inclined to take Jackie's side, was no doubt the supremely awkward moment when Kennedy found himself assuring Gunilla's mother that he had every intention of divorcing his wife so that he could marry her daughter. If 22-year old Jackie's dream of a happy, uncomplicated marriage to a promiscuous man 12 year her senior had been naïve, it was at least more dignified than the 37-year old Jack's dashed adolescent hopes for a week of anonymous sexual bliss with a girl he had only laid eyes on once.

The Democratic convention of 1956

Despite the fact that his marriage to Jackie had been critical to Kennedy's future in politics, she was not, at first, made privy to the full scope of his political ambitions. She knew that his father wanted him to run for president, but she didn't know when Kennedy planned to make his move. Considering that he was still in his late 30s, barely over the Constitutionally required age of 36, she may well have assumed that he intended to serve many more years in the Senate before making his bid. Yet, sometimes, she would overhear snatches of conversation through doorways, as Kennedy and his father plotted one strategic move or another, that roused her curiosity and hinted of big things right around the corner. Such matters were never discussed around the dinner table, however, or even in private, at least with her.

It was during the summer of 1956, amidst the run-up to the Democratic National Convention, that Kennedy first began seriously contemplating a shift from the legislative to the executive branch of American government. Everyone knew that Governor Adlai Stevenson would receive his party's nomination to run for a second time against Republican president Dwight Eisenhower, but the second slot on the Democratic ticket had yet to be filled. The idea that Kennedy, then a 39-year old junior senator who had only served one term, might take the vice-presidential slot, seemed absurd to many. But as soon as Kennedy realized that Stevenson's people were looking seriously at him, he decided that the vice-presidency was something he wanted very much, despite the fact that Joseph Kennedy thought that Stevenson was likely to be defeated, and that being the running-mate of an unsuccessful candidate would hurt Jack's chances at winning the presidency some day. Jackie, who was not informed that her husband was angling to make her Second Lady, nonetheless overheard so many suggestive remarks to that effect as to make her question Kennedy directly. He merely laughed at her.

Kennedy came extremely close to securing the VP nomination in 1956. His loss to Tennessee senator Estes Kefauver was the first defeat of his political career, but historians tend to agree that Kennedy won more by losing than he would have by winning. Stevenson had made the unusual move of leaving the choice of his running-mate up to the convention delegates, rather than choosing one for himself. When it became clear that Kennedy was going to lose to Kefauver, he decided to make a gesture towards party unity by pulling out of the running. Jackie was sitting in the balcony, trying to conceal tears of disappointment, as Kennedy gave a short speech, asking for his supporters among the delegates to give Kefauver their votes:

"I want to take this opportunity first to express my appreciation to Democrats from all part of the country...who have been so generous and kind to me this afternoon. I think it proves, as nothing else could prove, what a strong and

united party the Democratic party truly is.
Secondly, I think what has happened today bears
out the good judgement of Governor Stevenson
that this issue should be taken to the floor of the
convention, because I believe that the
Democratic Party will go from this convention
far stronger for what we have done here today.
And therefore, ladies and gentlemen, recognizing
that this convention has selected a man who has
campaigned in all parts of the country, who has
worked entirely for the party, who will serve as
an admirable running mate to Governor
Stevenson, I hope that this convention will make
Estes Kefauver's nomination unanimous. Mr.
Chairman, I move that we suspend the rules and
make the nomination of Estes Kefauver by
acclamation."

By putting aside his own interests and asking his
party to give Kefauver their unanimous support,
Kennedy threw wide the doors of his own
political future. He was the breakout star of the

1956 convention, and his election as President four year later would not have been possible without the storm of positive publicity he gained from his performance there. Kennedy seemed to sense this; by the time he and his colleagues had adjourned from the convention center to a nearby restaurant to have dinner and talk matters over, he scarcely seemed to be disappointed at all by the loss of the VP slot. But Jackie, who had been left alone in their new home for months with no company and nothing to do but see her doctor, furnish the nursery, and wonder what precisely her husband was up to, had nonetheless grown extremely invested in the idea that her husband might become vice-president, and she was devastated by the convention's outcome. She was in tears at the dinner table, partly because of the disappointment of losing, partly because she knew that Jack had decided, again without consulting her, to take yet another vacation to the south of France, leaving her to prepare for the birth of their child alone. Kennedy was due to leave the country the very next morning, and he didn't intend to return until the beginning of September, a month before her due date.

Kennedy would later blame the "excitement" of the convention for what followed, though it seems likely that the agitation of having been kept in the dark for so long also played a part. The convention ended on August 17, 1956. Less than a week later, on August 23, Jackie began to experience heavy bleeding. She was rushed to the hospital, where a Caesarean section was performed, resulting in the delivery of a stillborn daughter, whom Jackie named Arabella. When Jackie awoke from the anesthesia, she found at her bedside, not her husband, who was still in the south of France and unreachable, but her brother in law, Bobby Kennedy. Jackie and Bobby had never been close before, but that was about to change. Bobby seemed to feel that it was his personal responsibility to make up for Jack's inexplicable absence and dereliction of duty.

It was Bobby Kennedy that Jackie first saw as she was coming out from under the anesthesia, and it was Bobby who had to tell Jackie that she had lost the baby. Bobby went on to make all the arrangements for the funeral, and Bobby assured their mother Rose that there was a perfectly reasonable explanation why no one could get Jack on the phone. A great deal of pre-emptive damage control was necessary to keep Jack's absence from turning into a scandal of epic proportions. It was bad enough that he was undoubtedly keeping the company of other women while his daughter was being buried and his wife was in the hospital recovering from a serious surgery. What was worse was that, even after the dire news finally reached him, he seriously contemplated remaining in France for another week or so—despite the fact August was nearly over, and starting in September his campaign obligations for Stevenson would leave him with virtually no time to spend alone with

Jackie. Kennedy only agreed to return home immediately when a friend advised him that "to do otherwise would be disastrous for his presidential hopes."

Arabella Kennedy was buried on August 25, 1956. On August 26, Jack Kennedy finally called his wife from Europe. On August 28, he returned to the country, and suddenly, it was as if he could not reach Jackie quickly enough. He encouraged his driver to run traffic lights and stop signs to reach the hospital faster, promising that he would "pay for any tickets." Possibly he was feeling a belated sense of guilt; possibly he felt ashamed of himself. Possibly, he wanted American newspapers to report that he had been in a frantic hurry to reach his wife's bedside. Or perhaps it had suddenly dawned on him that his failures as a husband might be hurtful to more than just Jackie's feelings. The timely reminder that he could scuttle his presidential ambitions if he was seen to be neglecting his family may well have reminded him of an important truth. His career in the Senate would not have been possible if not for his marriage to Jackie Bouvier. And by the same token, his political career could implode in an instant if Jackie chose to leave him. There now seemed every chance that she might do so. She was furious, deeply depressed, and she feared that after losing two children (she had suffered a miscarriage in 1954, just before Jack's first back surgery) she might never have more. She was fearful, uncertain what the future might hold for her, and at her darkest hour, her husband had been in the south of France, sleeping with other women. A considerable degree of resentment was completely justified.

The fact of the matter was that Jack needed Jackie more than Jackie needed him. Regardless, he had treated her like an afterthought, keeping her in the dark about his work and his plans for the future. He was a serial adulterer, and despite all that Jackie had done for him, he had repeatedly made it clear that she was far down his list of priorities. Joseph Kennedy, who was himself compulsively unfaithful to his wife Rose, had served Jack poorly as a role model for marriage. Perhaps Jack thought that he, like his father, could do as he liked, and Jackie, like Rose, would always turn a blind eye. But Joseph and Rose Kennedy were bound, if by nothing else, by the nine children they shared. After Arabella's death, there was nothing to tying Jackie to Jack, nothing to stop her from walking away from her miserably unhappy marriage. If she had been blindly in love with Jack as a girl of 22, she was, after several years as his wife, blind no longer. Whether or not she loved him still remained to be seen.

Road to the White House

It had taken the Kennedys years to acquire a home of their own. In the early days of their marriage, after returning from their honeymoon, Jack had taken Jackie back to the Kennedy homestead in Hyannis Port, where they shared the same small, poky bedroom he had lived in as a little boy. Jack didn't seem to be in any particular hurry to establish a separate residence, but Jackie longed for the two of them to have a home of their own. They had briefly rented a house in Georgetown, then lived for awhile in hotels. After Jackie discovered she was pregnant, she had purchased a house in Virginia called Hickory Hill, which seemed to her like the perfect place to raise a child. But in 1956, in the aftermath of the stillbirth, Jackie found that she could not bear to return to the house where she'd spent so many hours lovingly furnishing a nursery for the child she had been forced to bury. She ended up selling Hickory Hill to Bobby and Ethel Kennedy shortly after her release from the hospital. In November of 1956, she spent a month abroad with her sister—choosing, for once, to be the person who created the distance in her marriage. Rumors began to spread in

Washington that the Kennedys' marriage was troubled and that they were rarely seen together because they had secretly decided to separate. Word had gotten out around Washington that Jack had been gallivanting in the south of France while his wife was in the hospital, and that he'd missed his own daughter's funeral. The most tantalizing rumor of all claimed that Joseph Kennedy, in an effort to head off a scandal that could ruin his son's career, had paid Jackie a million dollars to remain in the marriage.

The story was easy to believe because there were so many reasons for it to be true. But even though Jackie was by now painfully aware of the extent of her husband's philandering, there was no foundation to the rumors that the couple had separated. If anything, their marriage might almost have been said to be flourishing for the first time. By early 1957, Jackie was again pregnant, while Jack had made the decision to seriously pursue the Democratic nomination for the 1960 presidential election. Jackie still was not completely reconciled to her husband's waywardness, but she was fully committed to their marriage and to Jack's career.

Jack was by Jackie's side as she raced to the hospital to say goodbye to her father when Jack Bouvier succumbed to liver cancer in August of 1957. Their relationship improved still more after the birth of their daughter Caroline in November of that year. Jack proved to be a doting father, and for a time played the role of attentive husband to the hilt, not just in front of cameras, but in private as well. When the young family was featured on the cover of *Life* magazine the next year, their smiling faces were, for once, not merely a façade put on for the benefit of Jack's public image. Family and friends alike all noted that Jack was a natural as a father. "I don't think he really knew what loving someone was like until he had Caroline," one person observed. "He was adorable with her from the beginning."

By 1958, the Kennedys had purchased a family home in Georgetown, and as Jack prepared for his presidential bid, Jackie prepared to support him in the best way she knew how. This involved apprenticing herself to the tutelage of Washington political host and back room power broker, Joe Alsop—the very man who had ceased inviting Jack to his famous dinner parties six years earlier, because Kennedy had complained about the lack of pretty girls. Back then, Alsop had deemed Kennedy "not serious" enough to merit the privilege of admission to the closely vetted milieu of Washington insiders he presided over. He had only changed his mind after Kennedy's marriage to Jackie.

Jackie presented herself to Alsop—a figure marked by cultivated eccentricities, who smoked cigarettes from a long holder, affected a faux British accent of varying consistency, and boasted close family connections to both Theodore and Franklin Roosevelt—in the light of a student eager to learn his craft. In other words, she wanted Alsop to teach her how to be the same kind of gracious, formidable, all-knowing political host he was. In Washington, much of the real work of government was done off the floor of Congress, around the dinner tables of hosts like Joe Alsop, who made a point of bringing together only the people who mattered. As Jack's wife, Jackie was in a position to materially further her husband's interests by making her home a place where important men could dine with their wives, then leave them safely in their hostess's hands while they adjourned to a separate room to discuss business over brandy and cigars.

But Jackie was a neophyte by Washington standards, and Alsop would have to train her up considerably if she was to be an effective Washington political hostess. "At the outset," writes one biographer, "[Alsop] saw Jackie as a 'starter' who despite anything she had done or endured to date was suddenly at the very beginning of the particular race she had been designated to run in life. He judged that of all the starters he had seen and worked with in the course of his career, there had never previously been another who merited, in his phrase, 'a higher handicap.' Despite her immense potential, however, he also perceived that she possessed nowhere nearly enough self-confidence. That was where Joe came in."

Alsop was deeply invested in Jackie's success. As the mentor and protégé of the wife of the man who might well be president in 1960, he stood to gain a great deal from making himself indispensable to her. She had a "high role" to play in history, he judged. His tutelage involved lessons in food, wine, place settings, fashion, and furniture, as well as power and politics. He had known many young political wives like her, and by telling Jackie stories about how they had overcome challenges similar to the ones she was facing, he was able to encourage her when she became frustrated. Soon, Jackie and Alsop were constant companions.

Under Alsop's tutelage, Jackie transformed from a "sloppy kid", as one of her friends had once described her, into a chic, sophisticated purveyor of taste, with a strong preference for French fashions and furnishings. The goal of all her labors was to make herself a stronger political asset to her husband. It was therefore rather distressing to her when the Kennedy camp began debating whether ordinary Americans were "ready" for Jackie. There was concern that she was too sophisticated to appeal to American voters. In Jack's words, Jackie had "too much status and not enough quo". She was "fey and fancy"—not eccentric, precisely, but marked by her wealth, and sophisticated in a way that contrasted sharply with, for instance, Mamie Eisenhower's homespun housewife image.

There was also her sly, cutting sense of humor to consider. At times her remarks came across as too arch, a little too clever, for most reporters to cope with. They took her at face value when she was only being witty, and this contributed to her mercurial image. After all the work Jackie had put into cultivating a sophisticated fashion sense, she came under fire in the press for favoring French designers instead of buying her clothes at Macy's or Bloomingdales, like a good American housewife. Alsop had to counsel her that it might be a good idea to invite reporters along on a shopping trip where she purchased maternity clothes at a New York department store, and Jackie agreed, though she found the exercise absurd. When the reporters asked her whether there was any truth to the rumors that she spent upwards of $30,000 on clothes from the house of Givenchy, she retorted, both irritated and amused, that that would be impossible unless all her underwear were made of sable fur.

It is perhaps somewhat ironic that the very qualities which are now considered to have made Jackie Kennedy an iconic First Lady—her exquisite fashion sense, the knowledge of furnishings and antiquities that would enable her to restore the grandeur of the White House and open it to the public as a living museum of American history—were once seen as potential liabilities to her husband's image. But despite the fact that people sometimes responded badly to her bouffant hairdo and couturier costumes, she proved to an effective presence on the rare occasions when she joined Jack on the campaign trail. She didn't enjoy campaigning very much, as the large crowds and the necessity of making inoffensive conversation with hundreds of strangers strained her nerves and made her feel out of her element. Yet her natural inwardness translated on camera as a sweet, appealing shyness. Observers began to notice that when Jack and Jackie worked opposite sides of the aisle, the larger crowds tended to gather on Jackie's side.

First Lady

"Later," writes biographer Barbara Leaming, "Jackie would tell the story of her marriage to Jack Kennedy in terms of his evolving sense of her political viability—a process that, as she saw it, was not complete until the very last hours of his life. 'I had worked so hard at the marriage,' she told the Rev. Richard T. McSorley, a Jesuit priest who counseled her after the assassination. 'I had made an effort and succeeded and he had really come to love me and to congratulate me on what I did for him...It took a very long time for us to work everything out, but we did, and we were about to have a real life together. I was going to campaign with him."

When Kennedy defeated Republican candidate Richard Nixon in the 1960 presidential election, he and Jackie had only been married for seven years. She was pregnant during the final leg of the campaign, though she had delayed announcing it for as long as possible, fearful that she might have another miscarriage and thus be subjected to endless newspaper articles evaluating her obstetric health—at least one reporter had already made the subject of Jackie's pregnancies something of a specialty subject. Much to Jackie's relief, her son, John, was born healthy on November 25, 1960, only two weeks after Jack had become president-elect. The birth had followed a tense, unhappy Thanksgiving holiday, during which Jack had railed at Jackie over some misconstrued remarks that her newly-engaged press secretary had made to reporters. He'd left for Palm Beach the next day, but was forced to turn around almost immediately: Jackie had been rushed to the hospital with contractions and was undergoing another Caesarean section. Just as the upset at the 1956 Democratic convention had led to Jackie going into premature labor with Arabella, the fight over Thanksgiving dinner had sent Jackie into premature labor with John.

The couple's first son was born with underdeveloped lungs, and had to be placed in an incubator for the two weeks of his life. Jack remained in Washington the entire time, giving his family as much attention as possible until the danger was past. Things had changed in the Kennedy marriage since 1956; Jack was president now, and could not afford to be seen as anything less than a devoted husband and father. The birth weakened Jackie considerably, but as soon as she was released from the hospital, she was forced to accept an invitation from Mamie Eisenhower to come to the White House for a tour. Mrs. Eisenhower had come under considerable criticism for not extending the invitation earlier, and her aides were insistent that Jackie come as soon as possible, even though she was due to fly the Florida later that day. The Eisenhower people had assured Jackie that a wheelchair would be available for her, but through some oversight, no wheelchair was provided, and she was forced to complete the entire tour on foot. Afterwards, on the plane, she collapsed and was prescribed two weeks of bedrest. When Jack was sworn into office on January 20, 1961, Jackie was still ill and tired, and suffering from mild postpartum depression.

Both Kennedys suffered from serious bouts of ill health during their time in the White House, a fact which had to be concealed from the public, considering that they were supposed to embody youth and strength. Jack, as usual, was often in pain with his back, while Jackie suffered from fits of nervous exhaustion and muscle spasms in her legs. They both began to rely on the services of a German doctor, Max Jacobson, whose celebrity clients referred to him as "Doctor Feelgood". Jacobson provided his patients with injections of a secret drug cocktail, which included methamphetamine, steroids, calcium, and monkey placenta, including other ingredients he refused to disclose. Scolding those who reveled in the euphoric sensations his injections induced, Jacobson said, "it's not for kicks, only for people who have work to do." The long term health effects of such injections would no doubt have done a great deal more harm than good, but they allowed the Kennedys to put on a display of youthful vigor, charm, and effervescence, even when they were close to folding under the strain of their duties.

Jacobson's injections were at least partially responsible for the tremendous success of Jackie's first important moment as First Lady. (Jackie was uncomfortable with the title of "First

Lady"; she said that it sounded like the name of a saddle horse.) In May of 1961, the Kennedys made their historic visit to France, where relations with the U.S. had long been prickly. Rather to the astonishment of both Kennedy and the French president, Charles de Gaulle, more than a million people lined up along the streets to watch their motorcade pass, crying out "Vive Jacqueline!" Pharmaceutical assistance was keeping her energy up, certainly, but the immediate enthusiasm for her arrival in the country was due to an interview Jackie had given to French television reporters in Washington a few weeks earlier. It had been aired in France only the night before. In the interview, Jackie had spoken eloquently, in French, of the pride she took in her French ancestry, the pleasant time she had spent in Paris when she was studying at the Sorbonne, and her longstanding interest in French history. The French people responded with open adulation.

And it wasn't only the crowds that adored her. De Gaulle had been Jackie's childhood hero, but over the course of the visit, Jackie seemed to become rather a hero of de Gaulle's. The French president had issued stern criticism of Kennedy after the Bay of Pigs fiasco the previous month; now, he fondly informed Kennedy that his wife had a better grasp of French history than most Frenchwomen. Political talks between Kennedy and de Gaulle met with greater success than White House staff had anticipated, and Kennedy told his aides that it was "probably because I have such a charming wife." After Jackie made bold headlines by appearing at the Palace of Versailles in a white satin evening gown designed by Givenchy, Kennedy told a crowd, "I do not think it altogether inappropriate to introduce myself to this audience. I am the man who accompanied Jacqueline Kennedy to Paris, and I have enjoyed it." Unlike the Prince of Wales, who also found himself being eclipsed by his wife during their first tour of Australia and New Zealand, Kennedy's minor annoyance at playing second fiddle to Jackie was subsumed by his pragmatic awareness that he could only benefit from her popularity. After leaving France, the Kennedys went on to meet with Soviet leader Nikita Khrushchev in Vienna, where the Austrian people seemed to appear to be trying to outdo the French in their enthusiasm for greeting the American First Lady. Likewise, she was almost as popular in London, where the Kennedys attended the christening of Jackie's nephew Anthony, the first child of her sister Lee's marriage to Polish prince Stanislas Radziwill.

Upon their return to the United States, Jackie found that she had been transformed overnight into her husband's most valuable public relations asset. This was of crucial importance in the wake of the Bay of Pigs scandal, and the crises yet to come. The trip to London had been, in part, a disguised opportunity for Kennedy to speak with British leadership about his conversation with

Khrushchev in Vienna. The Soviet premier had informed Kennedy that he was preparing to cut off western access to East Berlin, rather than allow Germany to unite once more as an anti-Communist power, and he would persist in his intention even if it ignited a third World War. Kennedy had been left deeply shaken by the conversation, and feared, correctly as it turned out, that he had appeared weak in Khrushchev's eyes.

Since Kennedy's assassination, the American people have consistently ranked John F. Kennedy as one of the greatest presidents in history. Historians, however, have never honored him with this distinction, nor was Kennedy considered to be an especially effective president when he was alive. The fact that he is remembered so fondly today has more to do with the combined mythmaking efforts of Jackie and the Kennedy family than with anything he accomplished while in office. And it is likely that the Kennedy legend—Camelot, as Jackie would famously dub it—could never have been so effectively inscribed on the American consciousness, if not for the enormous of amount of social capital that Jackie garnered prior to the assassination, and the skillful way she drew on it during the aftermath. The Kennedy legend effectively began with Jackie Kennedy's trip to France, though it would be years before anyone realized it.

Chapter Four: Dallas

The death of John F. Kennedy

The Cuban Missile Crisis of 1962 was a period of abject terror for both President Kennedy and the First Lady. On Kennedy's part, he felt personally responsible for Khrushchev's decision to build missile bases in Cuba; during their talks in Vienna, Kennedy believed that he had given Khrushchev the impression that he was weak-willed and vacillating, likely to agree to any number of appeasement gestures if it would help to avoid the threat of another war breaking out. Khrushchev's plan was to travel to America personally and demand huge concessions in Germany from the West after the missile sites had been completed. Throughout the tense stand-off that followed, when it seemed entirely possible that Russian nuclear missiles might fire on Washington at any moment, Jackie and Kennedy turned to each other for comfort, achieving a closeness that had never been present in their marriage before. Jackie begged Jack not to send her or the children away to a secure location. "Please don't send me anywhere," she said. "If anything happens, we're all going to stay right here with you. Even if there's not room in the bomb shelter in the White House, please then I just want to be with you, and I want to die with you, and the children do too—[rather] than live without you."

Not long after the crisis was averted, Jackie began to confide tentatively in a few close friends that she was once again pregnant. She had taken on a more active public role following the success of her European tour, hosting the hour-long program *A Television Tour of the White House with Mrs. John F. Kennedy*, a first of its kind glimpse inside the President's home, pitched to be accessible to everyday Americans who were unlikely to ever have the opportunity of touring the White House in person. In this documentary,

Jackie portrays herself skillfully as Housewife-in-Chief, drawing on her Miss Porter's training to graciously welcome viewers into her husband's home and invite them to regard it as their house as well—or rather, as a public museum that showcased their nation's history, past and present. Remarkably, Jackie did not speak from notes or from a teleprompter, even though the subject was complicated and the program lengthy. Her remarks were improvised on the spot, her natural eloquence obviating the need for a speechwriter's contributions.

During the pregnancy, however, she began to withdraw from public life. She'd already suffered a stillbirth and a miscarriage, and even her pregnancies with Caroline and John had been difficult, their births premature. This time, she didn't want to take any chances or subject herself to any avoidable strain. Despite all her precautions, however, Patrick Kennedy was, like his siblings, born prematurely. He had a fairly healthy birth weight of four pounds and ten ounces, but he also had a far more severe case of the same condition that had caused his older brother to be born with underdeveloped lungs. From the moment he was delivered, it cost him so much effort to breathe that his entire body quivered with each inhalation. Patrick was moved to Children's Hospital in Boston to be treated by specialists, while Jackie was forced to remained at Otis Air Force Base hospital in Cape Cod to recover from the C-section. She was only able to spend ten minutes with Patrick before he was rushed away.

On the night Patrick died, after only 39 hours of life, Jack Kennedy was sitting next to his bed in a white cap and gown; when he drew his last breath, his father was holding his hand. Jack immediately returned to Cape Cod to be with Jackie, where "he knelt by her bedside and sobbed". It was a display of emotion the likes of which Jackie had never seen in her husband before. He wept at the funeral as well, and before Patrick was lowered into the ground next to his stillborn sister Arabella, Jack placed his St. Christopher medal in the coffin with him. "He was a beautiful baby," the president told doctors after Patrick passed away. "He put up a hell of a fight." No doubt Jack was thinking of all the childhood illnesses he had suffered and fought through himself.

While Patrick was still fighting for his life, Jack, somewhat despairingly, told Jackie's mother that nothing must happen to the baby, because he feared Jackie wouldn't be able to bear it. He wasn't wrong; Jackie fell into an extremely deep depression in the weeks that followed. Her sister Lee invited her to take a boating holiday with her on a yacht owned by Greek millionaire Aristotle Onassis, a close friend of hers, in the hopes that getting away from Washington for a time would help her to recover.

There was considerable consternation both inside and outside the White House over the prospect of such a trip. Jackie had already been on one solo overseas vacation since Jack became president, and there had been public outcry after she was photographed seemingly alone on a yacht in the company of her male host. It was suggested that Jackie must be having an affair with the man—despite the fact that she had not, in fact, been alone with him or with any other man during her travels, and only appeared so in the photograph because of the suggestive way the photographer had framed the image, cutting out the crowd of other guests and Secret Service agents just behind her. Many Americans wrote to the White House to express the view that it wasn't right for the President's wife to spend so much time in Europe merely for her own pleasure, and that, if she must travel, she should make a tour of the United States instead. The fact that she was being accused of taking a luxury European cruise for the purpose of dallying with another man was especially galling to Jackie, who had always been faithful, because Kennedy flaunted his sexual encounters with other women to such an extent that even his close friends were beginning to grow disgusted with him. Drug and sex parties were so much a feature of life in the White House that Betty Coxe Spaulding, a close friend of the Kennedys, later remarked, "They had turned that place into a brothel, hadn't they?"

The idea that Jackie might be having an extramarital affair of her own struck many people as believable, because it seemed not unlikely that the wife of such a faithless husband might be looking to fight fire with fire. But Jackie's own Secret Service agents put paid to that notion; having watched all of her interactions with men for several years, they declared her "above that sort of thing". Jack himself was irritated by the negative publicity, but he didn't blame Jackie for it. And now, in the wake of Patrick's death, he overrode the objections of his aides, and even his brother Bobby, who served as his attorney general, that the trip could severely damage his image. He told Jackie that she should go on vacation with her sister if she wanted to; she deserved a break, and he hoped that the time away would help to lift her spirits. But the backlash against this vacation was even more considerable than it had been the last time. Journalists and letter-writers alike seemed to feel that, if Jackie was sufficiently recovered from her C-section and her son's death to go on yet another foreign yachting holiday, then she was recovered enough to stay at home and go back to her duties as First Lady.

Patrick had died on August 3, 1963; Jackie did not return to the country until October 3. When she returned, she was mortified to discover how much embarrassment she had caused her husband's administration by remaining away for "much longer than necessary", as she put it. Of the last five months of Jack's life, Jackie spent almost three of them abroad. After his death, Jackie would bitterly regret that she had missed the chance to be with him as much as possible.

In November of 1963, all of Jack's thoughts were fixed upon the upcoming election. He was planning an extensive tour of the country as part of his re-election campaign, and this time, unlike during the 1960 election, he invited Jackie to come with him. It would do the country good to see the President and his wife sitting side by side and smiling together, and might even put an end to the grumbling that Jackie wasn't sufficiently attentive to her duties—not to mention the persistent rumors that their marriage was falling apart. Jackie had never been comfortable on the campaign trail. She was intimidated by the crowds that amassed to see her husband during public appearances, never quite certain what she ought to say to the strangers who wanted to shake her hand and ask her questions. But she felt guilty about the trouble her vacation had caused him, so when Jack invited her to join him on a visit to Texas in late November, she agreed. It was "a gesture of contrition" on her part, though she had scarcely done anything wrong. But that was the pattern of their marriage: any time there was any sort of conflict between them, Jackie was the first to make a conciliating gesture.

Just as in 1956, there was still some concern amongst the Kennedy camp that the American public wouldn't take well to Jackie. She took these concerns at face value, and attempted to make herself inoffensive to Texans by dressing, and behaving, rather like the wife of a well to do American businessman, rather than the chic coutured sophisticate the newspapers made her out to be. During the first stop of the Texas trip, in San Antonio, Jackie won people over with what Lady Bird Johnson, wife of then vice-president Lyndon Johnson, who had accompanied them, called her "big, hesitant smile". Jackie hoped to send the message that, even if the people of France had once greeted her with shouts of "Vive Jacqueline", she wasn't taking it for granted that the people of Texas would automatically give her their full-throated approval. She wasn't looking to repeat her European triumph. Her only hope for her visit was that her presence would help Jack.

Yet, in San Antonio, the crowds proved just as wild for her as they had been in Paris or Vienna or London. Jack was, for once, quick to take notice and reward her with his approval. "Two years ago," he told a Texas crowd, "I introduced myself in Paris by saying that I was the man who accompanied Mrs. Kennedy to Paris. I am getting the same sensation as I travel about Texas." That night, in their hotel room, Jack asked Jackie to join him in two weeks when he made his next campaign trip, this time to California. He no longer had any reservations about whether or not America was prepared to embrace her. "Henceforward," writes one biographer, "when he went on the road, he wanted Jackie at his side."

The events of November 22, 1963 scarcely need to be described in detail to anyone who has ever viewed the famous Zapruder film, which depicts the assassination with vivid, horrifying clarity. But there are some moments which the film, which was shot from a considerable distance, did not capture. The sound of the first bullet fired was taken to be the sound of a backfiring motorcycle; there were several policemen on motorcycles at the head of motorcade. The second shot, however, passed through Kennedy's neck and struck Texas governor John Connally in the shoulder. Jackie heard the shot, but did not turn to look, thinking it was another backfire. Not until she heard Connally gasp, "My God, they are going to kill us all," did she turn to see Jack with his hand at his throat, blood welling between his fingers. She would blame herself, afterwards, for having been looking in the opposite direction when he was shot the first time; she believed she might have been able to protect him from the second bullet if she'd only had a few more seconds.

Immediately, she began trying to pull Jack down in the seat to take cover, as Governor Connally's wife was doing next to her. Unlike Connally, however, Jack was rigid, held upright by the stiff back brace he wore, and Jackie wasn't strong enough to make him bend. Five long seconds passed—and then the third gunshot fired, and Kennedy was struck by the second bullet. Jackie's face was inches from her husband's when the bullet tore through his skull. Instantly, she was showered in blood, brain matter, and bone shards. As Jack fell towards her, Jackie, fully aware that she was making herself a target should the gunman fire a fourth shot, started to climb over the back of the open vehicle. In the Zapruder film, it appears that she is attempting to grab the hand of Clint Hill, the lead Secret Service agent in her personal detail, who was running after the car. But Hill later said that he didn't think Jackie even noticed him at first. He believed she was reaching for a piece of her husband's skull that had been blown off by the gunshot. Other nearby agents feared that she was going to fall out of the car and land under the tires of the oncoming vehicles. At last, she grasped Hill's hand, and Hill climbed into the car, pushing her down in the seat and covering both Jackie and the President with his own body. Pressed under his weight, Jackie cradled her husband's head in her lap with both hands pressed to the gaping hole at the back of his head. She was trying to keep what was left of brain inside of what remained of his skull. When she reached the hospital, she would still be clutching a large skull fragment. In a dazed state, she presented it to a doctor, as though she thought there was a chance that he might be able to reattach it.

It took six minutes for the motorcade to reach the hospital after Kennedy was struck in the head. When doctors tried to transfer Kennedy onto the stretcher, Jackie refused to let any of the medical staff touch his head, as though she had convinced herself that by applying pressure to the hole she was keeping Jack alive. She ran alongside the stretcher as he was wheeled into the trauma room. The doctors who greeted the president's limousine had taken one look at the quantity of blood and brain matter visible on the seats and concluded that the president must be dead already. Yet, incredibly, Kennedy was still breathing. Jackie fell to her knees next to his bed and began to pray, the way she had prayed for him after his back surgery years earlier after the doctors had told her he would not live out the night. Eventually, she was persuaded to leave the room, and the trauma doctors began to perform chest compressions. Each time pressure was applied to Kennedy's chest, a gout of blood shot through the wound in his skull. It took the arrival of the consulting neurologist to persuade the trauma team to cease the compressions. There was no point, he explained; no one could survive head trauma of such magnitude. A priest was called, and last rites were performed. Jackie returned to the room and once again knelt beside the bed to pray. Then she went out into the corridor to wait.

There was a rush to get Kennedy's body out of the hospital. State officials were insisting that the autopsy must be performed in Texas, since that was where the murder had taken place. But now that the President was dead, Jackie Kennedy was the chief focus of the Secret Service agents' concern. One agent summed up everyone's worries: "I'm concerned that the Dallas police are going to come and take the body off the plane and Jackie Kennedy's going to have a heart attack right in front of us there. I'm petrified." But when they reached Air Force One, the delay in take-off came, not from the Dallas police, but from the pilot. Lyndon Baines Johnson was now President of the United States, and Air Force One could not take off without his order. Before that happened, Johnson wanted to be officially sworn in, even though, legally, he had become president the moment Kennedy was declared dead.

After Johnson's swearing in, which Jackie attended still wearing her blood soaked pink suit, there was a moment of banal confusion. Jackie tried to retreat to her bedroom, only to discover that, since it was the presidential suite, it had already been given over to the Johnsons. Jackie rushed to the back of the plane to sit next to Jack's coffin again, before the Johnsons found her and insisted that she keep the room while the plane was en route to Washington.

An aide had lain a change of clothes out on the bed so that Jackie could clean up. There was so much blood on her clothing that her stockings, gloves, and sleeves were completely saturated. But as she stood regarding herself in the bathroom mirror, she decided that she would not change clothes. She started to wipe the blood off her face, then stopped. In the hospital, where Jack's body had been placed in a coffin, she had removed her wedding ring so that she could place it on her husband's finger. In order to do so, she'd had to remove her gloves, but they were so stiff with blood that she'd had to ask a doctor to help her work them off her hands. Lady Bird Johnson came to sit with Jackie a few minutes later. She found herself marveling at the sight of the elegantly dressed woman who looked as though she had just emerged from a war zone. She too suggested that Jackie put on clean clothes, but Jackie was adamant: "I want them to see what they have done to Jack," she said. She spent the rest of the flight sitting next to Jack's coffin.

The Widow of Camelot

When Air Force One touched down at Andrew's Air Force Base, Bobby Kennedy, who had been waiting out of sight of reporters at the back of a military aircraft, suddenly ran across the tarmac and burst into the plane, pushing past the newly sworn-in president and his wife. "Where's Jackie?" he demanded. "I want to be with Jackie." Told that she was with the coffin, Bobby ran to her side and pulled her into an embrace. It was the first time she had allowed anyone to hug her or give her comfort since the nightmare began. Bobby had arranged for a helicopter to remain on standby so she could be transported directly to the White House while Kennedy's body was being transferred to Bethesda Naval Hospital for the autopsy. But once again, Jackie refused to be parted from Jack. Barbara Leaming describes the effect that Jackie's appearance produced when at last she stepped out of the plane and into the sight of the the reporters and photographers who had gathered there in anticipation of this very moment:

"When at length she emerged into the lights and cameras on the tarmac, onlookers wept at the sight of her befouled garments and thousand-yard stare. The blood on the pink wool spoke to the suddenness of the tragedy and the impermanence of earthly dominion. Everything she had painstakingly created and made herself known for had been snatched away in an instant."

Bobby remained by Jackie's side as they rode to the hospital. Staring sightlessly at a patch of grey curtain next to her brother in law's head, she told him the whole story, starting from the moment she heard the first bullet, to the moment they loaded the coffin onto Air Force One. In her almost trancelike state, she would spend the rest of the day repeating the story by rote in all its grim detail to anyone who sat with her for long enough to listen, including Secretary of Defense Robert McNamara, who found himself kneeling at her feet for over an hour. She emphasized, over and over again, how she had held Jack's head in her hands, how she had tried to hold his brain inside his shattered skull. The people she spoke to didn't necessarily want to hear all of these details, but everyone agreed that she seemed to need to say them out loud, as though she were trying to understand herself what she had just experienced.

Even though Jackie looked as though almost all the life had been drained out of her, she resisted the efforts of everyone who tried to take care of her. People urged her to rest, but she couldn't sleep, and refused to be sedated. It had now been many hours since the gunshots rang out over Dallas, but still, Jackie refused to change her clothes. Meanwhile, Bobby Kennedy was making arrangements for Jack's funeral. As President Kennedy's younger brother, and rather more officially as his attorney general, he had been giving orders in Jack's name for a long time. Now he was giving orders in Jackie's name. Jackie would want things done properly, he insisted. Jackie would want this church, these flowers, these readings. Left behind at the hospital, Jackie was at last persuaded by her doctor to let him inject her with a strong sedative. He anticipated she would be asleep within ten minutes. Instead, she continued to remain wide awake for hours. This was the beginning of the insomnia that would continue to plague her for a long time to come.

Now, 54 years after the assassination, it is easy to forget that Americans under the Kennedy administration faced a very real and present threat of nuclear attack by the Soviets. Lyndon Johnson believed there was a strong possibility that the assassination was the precursor to a large-scale attack on the United States, or even that Soviet plants inside the government itself had conspired to kill the President. These suspicions seemed even more credible after the apprehension and arrest of Lee Harvey Oswald, who, it was quickly discovered, had spent thirty-two months in the Soviet Union. Though Johnson later took criticism for his actions, this was the reason why he had insisted on being sworn in as President before Air Force One left Dallas; if there was a conspiracy in place, he felt that the best way to thwart it was with a clear demonstration that the government was stable and the American people still had a President.

If a large-scale follow up attack was going to take place, the logical time and place for it to happen would be at Kennedy's funeral. Jackie had announced her intention to walk behind Jack's coffin during the funeral procession, following it from the White House to St. Matthew's church, where the funeral would take place. If the widowed First Lady intended to walk behind the coffin, many other high-ranking officials would feel obliged to join her, including President Johnson, Bobby Kennedy, French president Charles de Gaulle, and the Soviet emissary representing Nikita Khrushchev. So many western world leaders gathered in a single place would make a tempting target for any assassin. And even if no attack was forthcoming against people like de Gaulle or Johnson, the rumors of suspected Soviet involvement in Kennedy's death might lead to a vengeful assault on the Soviet emissary, which would provoke another diplomatic crisis between Washington and Moscow.

Jackie was unmoved by these concerns. When she was told that other dignitaries would feel obliged to walk the eight blocks to the church if she did, Jackie replied: "They can ride or do whatever they want to. I'm walking behind the president to St. Matthew's." Charles de Gaulle likewise refused to ride in a car, even though he had already survived nine assassination attempts, and had received a death threat the very morning of the funeral. "I shall walk with Mrs. Kennedy," he said simply.

Chapter Five: Aftershocks

Cape Cod

Joseph Kennedy had suffered a massive stroke in 1961 which left him mostly paralyzed, bed-bound, and thus unable to attend his son's funeral. When Jackie left Washington, her immediate destination was the Kennedy home at Cape Cod, where Joseph lived surrounded by his family and cared for round the clock by a professional nurse. Over the objections of his wife and children, Jackie made straight for Joseph's bedroom upon her arrival. Sitting by his side, holding his hand, she recounted to him the same story she had told his son Bobby and numerous other people on November 22. The possibility that her ailing, aged father in law might not wish to hear the graphic details of how his son's skull had been shattered by a bullet did not seem to occur to her. The "post" phase of Jackie's looming post-traumatic stress disorder had not yet begun to set in. She was still in the grip of the trauma itself, reliving it daily, with perfect recall of the events she had witnessed and participated in. The aftermath was still to come; for Jackie, the assassination was still very much her present reality.

While staying with the Kennedys, Jackie surprised everyone by summoning a journalist from *Life* magazine to come to Cape Cod and take an interview with her. Theodore H. White had previously written an admiring book about Kennedy's presidential campaign, and for this reason Jackie judged him to be sympathetic to her goal, which was to leave the American people with an abiding positive impression of the president Kennedy had been. On the phone with White, she expressed concern that other journalists—people who had been hostile to her husband's administration—were about to start writing their own critical post-mortem analyses of his career. She wanted to get her own perspective on Jack's presidency out to the world, to set the tone for how he would be remembered by history, before such criticisms could be leveled.

When Kennedy was alive, even when their relationship was at its rockiest, Jackie had always been her husband's staunchest defender. Kennedy would shrug off insults and betrayals alike, never taking slights personally. Jackie, by contrast, met any disloyalty to her husband with unbridled fury, of a sort that inspired one biographer to describe her as Kennedy's "one-woman Praetorian Guard". Two weeks after his death, it was a duty she had not yet resigned. White and his editors were astonished that Jackie was offering to give them an interview; everyone had assumed that the last thing the grieving widow would wish to do was speak to the press so soon after the assassination. But once the offer had been made, there was no question of turning her down. So eager were

White's editors to print the first exclusive interview with the former First Lady that publication of the first December issue of *Life* was put on hold until White could reach Cape Cod and hear what she had to say.

Jackie's interview with White began when Jackie asked him, "How can I help you?", as though he had been the one to ask for her time, and not the other way around. White responded by asking Jackie how she wanted Jack to be remembered. The start of the conversation was vague, meandering—and then, to White's astonishment, she switched tracks abruptly and without pause, and began sharing with him the story she had told Bobby Kennedy, Robert McNamara, Joseph Kennedy, and many others. There was more gruesome detail in it than White wanted to hear, certainly more than he could print. The final, published version of White's article was no doubt shocking enough to the readers of the time, but it was a drastically condensed and sanitized version of the story that Jackie had told him. He was astonished by the level of detail she could remember, but most of those details would have been too much for the American public to bear.

The first half of White's article is the story of what happened in Dallas on November 22. In this section, White paraphrased Jackie's comments rather than quoting her directly. He began with the first gunshot, mistaken for a motorcycle's backfire; he alluded to the blood that stained the seats of the limousine, without specifying what a copious amount of blood it was, and left out entirely any mention of brain matter or bone shards. He mentioned the bouquet of red roses lying on the seat between Jack and Jackie, a gift from the people of Dallas, and how the roses were crushed in the confusion, scattering their petals everywhere, red rose petals mingling with the red blood. White began to quote Jackie's own words in the second half of the short article, when she began speaking to the question he had asked her at the first: how did she want her husband to be remembered? And that was when Jackie presented him with the image which, today, still defines the Kennedy presidency for many people: the image of Camelot.

"When Jack quoted something, it was usually classical," she said, "but I'm so ashamed of myself—all I keep thinking of is this line from a musical comedy." The musical comedy she was alluding to was the Broadway hit *Camelot,* starring Richard Burton as King Arthur and Julie Andrews as Queen Guinevere. Jack had often played the record before bed, and he was particularly fond of a line from the final song: "Don't let it be forgot, that once there was a spot, for one brief shining moment that was known as Camelot." Jackie spoke of Kennedy's boyhood illnesses, how he had passed the long hours of recovery reading about King Arthur, then later about historical heroes like Marlborough. She implied that, to her, Kennedy was cut from the same heroic cloth, and that she hoped his heroism would inspire other children as King Arthur and the rest had once inspired him. The Kennedy administration, in her eyes, was the Camelot of their era. And that was how she wanted Americans to remember it, and him.

Jackie spoke to White for three and a half hours, and at the conclusion of the interview, he was in a daze. He was given a spare room in the servants' quarters of the house to write in, and there he studied the notes he had taken. They were so disturbing to him that he was unable to transcribe them properly for another three and a half weeks, and even then he refused to show them to anyone, even his wife and his editors. When he sent the copy to Jackie, he advised her not to show them to anyone, with the possible exception of her brother in law, Bobby. The transcript was an invaluable contribution to the historical record, but the assassination itself was not yet history—many years would have to pass before anyone would be capable of reading Jackie's firsthand account with the detachment necessary for scholarship.

White's editors, who were losing money with every hour they delayed publication, waited impatiently for him to finish a draft of the interview. But before White could dictate his article to them over the phone, it had to pass Jackie's review. He was expecting her to make only a few comments or suggestions. Instead, she rewrote entire paragraphs, blacked out whole passages, added phrases, altered his wording. This would be her definitive statement to the world on Jack's death, and she was determined to exercise control over every syllable. When White at last produced a draft that met with Jackie's approval, the dominant feature was the Camelot metaphor. Jackie stood next to White as he spoke to his editors on the phone, and when they balked at the treacly sentimentality of the fairy tale image, Jackie was standing by, shaking her head. The Camelot metaphor would have to stay, White told his superiors. And so it did.

"Bleeding inside"

Post-traumatic stress disorder, or PTSD, did not yet exist as a psychiatric diagnosis in 1963. Its diagnostic ancestor, "shell-shock", was first recognized amongst soldiers who fought in the first World War, but the broader application to women and civilians who had experienced trauma in the course of everyday life was not recognized until the 1970s, when dialogue between the emerging women's movement and veterans of the war in Vietnam enabled psychologists to distinguish the similarities between the mental health symptoms experienced by survivors of sexual assault and survivors of wartime violence. PTSD was first officially recognized by the American

Psychological Association in the third edition of
the Diagnostic and Statistical Manuel of Mental
Disorders, or DSM-III, in 1980—some seventeen
years too late to be of use to Jackie Kennedy,
whose state of mind in the years following the
Kennedy assassination revealed textbook
symptoms of the condition.

Sufferers of post-traumatic stress disorder
usually struggle to remember the traumatic
events they experienced without reliving them at
the same time. Jackie suffered acutely from
uncontrollable, intrusive recollections of the
assassination, and she could not seem to help
sharing those recollections with friends,
strangers, government officials, anyone who
spent any significant amount of time in her
company. Everyone she spoke to felt that Jackie
had told them far more than they had ever
wanted to know, but no matter how many times
she repeated the story to them, they couldn't
bring themselves to cut her off, because she

seemed to need to talk about it. The truth was, she would have given anything to be able to *stop* talking about it. But talking about November 22 was the only relief she found from remembering November 22. The haunting doubts, the horrible images, the blood, the brains, and the bone shards, all of it filled her mind like a chorus of clamoring voices over which nothing else could be heard. Nothing could distract her from the assassination for long. The narrative of Dallas was overpowering her, because it did not yet belong to her. It belonged to some inexplicable external force which had swept into her life like a hurricane to take away everything she loved best.

The American public continued to picture Jackie as she had appeared at Kennedy's funeral, where, dazed, and on emotional lockdown, she had given a convincing performance of stoicism from behind the obscurity of her black mourning veil. People praised her for setting an example of courage for the nation. But every time Jackie heard someone praise her for her behavior during the funeral, she grew irritable. "How did they expect me to behave?" she demanded. Jackie came of a social class that did not lightly show emotion in public, and that early training in decorum had served her well. But it did not reflect the reality of her inner emotional state, and the tranquility she had displayed in public was not evident in her private life. People spoke of time healing all wounds as though healing were a natural process that would begin on its own. But Jackie knew perfectly well that she wasn't healing. And neither she nor anyone close to her was equipped to understand why.

Jackie's chief supporter, from the time of JFK's assassination until his own death in 1968, was Bobby Kennedy. One of Bobby's closest friends remarked that he had never seen a man more drastically altered by grief than Bobby was after the death of Jack. After Jackie, it was undoubtedly Bobby who felt Jack's lost most keenly. He lost an alarming amount of weight after the assassination; photographs of Kennedy's funeral procession showing Bobby next to his younger brother Teddy reveal the perfect fit of Ted's tailored morning suit, compared to the slackness in the fit of Bobby's. But unlike Jackie, who was struggling with something more profound than simple grief, Bobby used his feelings of loss to fuel his forward momentum. Always driven, always ready for a fight, Bobby Kennedy had been dubbed "Action Man" by his friends because of his energetic approach to crises. It was an energy that Jackie envied and admired. She asked herself why she couldn't be more like Bobby and Ethel, who were coping by throwing themselves into the work of upholding Jack's political legacy. But then, Bobby had his career to look after. Jackie, by contrast, had no career to take her mind off of things. Her career had been Jack's career, and Jack was gone.

Bobby's designated role in the Kennedy family business had always been to serve Jack's interests. Now that both of his older brothers were gone and his father was permanently incapacitated from the effects of stroke, Bobby had become the head of the extended Kennedy clan, a responsibility he had to shoulder in addition to being a father to his own family of ten children. Yet he made it his business to take responsibility for Jackie as well. Caring for his brother's widow was undoubtedly one of the most important outlets he had for his grief over his brother's death. Bobby was fiercely protective towards Jackie in the aftermath of the assassination. He'd been angered by the fact that Johnson insisted on being sworn into office before Air Force One left Dallas, because he felt that Johnson had deprived his brother of the honor of returning to Washington as President one final time. But this was nothing compared to his rage over the fact that Johnson had asked Jackie, who was in no condition to consent to anything, to stand next to him during his swearing-in. The now famous photograph of Jackie standing next to Johnson while he takes the oath of office, wearing her blood-soaked clothing and staring into the middle distance as though she doesn't quite know where she is, was proof, in Bobby's eyes, of Johnson's willingness to take advantage of her.

As JFK's widow, Jackie was now an even greater political asset than she had been as First Lady. While her husband was president, she had worked very hard to increase her value in this capacity, but that had been for Jack's benefit, not hers. After Jack's death, a kind of succession crisis ensued, almost medieval in its character. Who would inherit the imprimatur of the widow whose personal popularity and public relations cachet had so bolstered Kennedy's standing with the American people? Both Lyndon Johnson and Bobby Kennedy regarded themselves as Jack's rightful heirs in this regard. Johnson meant to step into Kennedy's shoes during the 1964 presidential election, so he needed Jackie beside him, both literally and metaphorically. Bobby Kennedy bitterly resented that Johnson had "used" Jackie at a moment when she was incapable of weighing these implications for herself, but he too would make considerable use of Jackie during his upcoming race for the Senate. Yet Bobby was not like Johnson; he was family. More to the point, Bobby would not ask Jackie for her help until many months after the assassination, compared to Johnson, who had asked Jackie to be photographed with him at the most vulnerable moment of her entire life.

Bobby saw his duty towards Jackie in terms of stepping into Jack's role as her guide and protector, though in reality, he had always been more sensitive to her feelings and attentive to her needs than Jack had been. He was simply a different sort of person than Jack. A devout Catholic and a devoted family man, Bobby was more sincere and more honest in his dealings with people, even the people he hated, than his older brother, who was considered secretive and manipulative, even by those who loved him. Jackie cared for Johnson, and regarded Johnson's oft-protested affection for her as sincere, but if it came to a choice between them, Jackie would always be Bobby's supporter first.

Bobby monitored Jackie's state of mind closely after she moved out of the White House and into a house provided for her by the State Department, which served as temporary lodgings until she purchased a home of her on N Street, in Georgetown, where she and Jack had lived together before he was elected President. The N Street house quickly became, first a pilgrimage site, and then a tourist attraction for the people of Washington. Crowds gathered outside of the house on a daily basis to hold candlelight vigils in memory of their slain president. Though Jackie rarely left the house, or indeed her bedroom, which was located on the second floor, she could not always avoid passing through the crowds. Understandably, large crowds of strangers terrified her after Dallas, especially since the distraught tourists often tried to speak to her, or touch her or her children, seeking comfort for their own grief by trying to "comfort" Kennedy's widowed family. She would not remain in the N Street house for very long before moving to New York, where she hoped she would be less easily recognized.

Jackie's nervousness around large crowds, like her insomnia, her persistent, intrusive memories of the assassination, and her avoidance of anything that reminded her too sharply of Kennedy or of Dallas, are all textbook symptoms of post-traumatic stress disorder. Yet in 1963, before PTSD was widely recognized and understood to be a common response to a trauma such as Jackie had undergone, her feelings and reactions were understood only as the grief that any woman would experience after becoming a widow so suddenly and so young. It would have been almost unthinkable to suggest that she required psychiatric intervention, even if the psychiatrists of the day had been equipped to help her, which is by no means certain. Back then, psychiatric treatment was perceived as being for crazy people, or degenerates—not for former First Ladies.

As a month passed, then three months, then six, with no sign of Jackie making progress, Bobby Kennedy turned for help, not to doctors, but to the more traditional options of friends, family, and the Church. British ambassador David Ormsby-Gore was one of the first people who were invited to assist Bobby in lifting Jackie's spirits. Ormsby-Gore had once been friends with Kathleen Kennedy and her husband Billy Hartington; after Kathleen's death, he and his family had taken the grieving Jack Kennedy under their wing in much the same way they now did for Jackie. After Jackie and Bobby, Ormsby-

Gore was probably the person who took Jack's death the hardest, so he and his wife Sissie devoted themselves to Jackie's cause with an energy. In addition to providing her with company and a listening ear, they were of help in more practical matters as well. When new premises had to be found for Caroline Kennedy's schoolroom after the family moved out of the White House, the Ormsby-Gores offered to host her and her teachers at the British embassy.

David Ormsby-Gore had been appointed to his ambassadorship by prime minister Harold Macmillan, who had also been close to Jack Kennedy. Jackie wrote a letter of condolence to Macmillan, with the intention of expressing how much her husband had loved and admired him. But as happened to her so often in those days, she found herself straying from her intended topic and pouring her anguish out on the page. She explained to Macmillan how the memories of November 22 kept recurring to her in all their vivid, "satin-red" detail. She questioned how God could have allowed such a senseless tragedy to take place. Jackie had expressed similar feelings many times before to other friends and acquaintances, but in this case, her correspondent was in a unique position to understand what she was suffering, and how that suffering differed from the grief of a tragic but more ordinary loss.

Harold Macmillan was a veteran of World War I, and having had his own taste of shell shock, he recognized it when he saw it in another. He wrote to her of his own experiences in the trenches, of losing practically every friend of his own generation to violent, senseless death in a violent, senseless war. He empathized with Jackie's bewilderment as to how God could countenance so much injustice and senseless waste. Above all, he validated the scope of Jackie's anguish. She wasn't being hysterical, or self-indulgent, he told her; she was reacting the way soldiers did when they returned from the battlefield to their homes and tried to go about the ordinary business of life again, only to find that that everything that once held meaning for them was now empty and hollow. In other words, Jackie wasn't alone in her feelings. They were a recognized phenomenon experienced by other people, and not, as some of her friends had suggested, evidence of self-indulgence on her part.

Jackie reread Macmillan's letter countless times. It became a bedrock for her, a source of comfort when she awoke from screaming nightmares in the middle of the night, or entertained doubts as to whether Caroline and John would not be better off if she too were to die. She struggled to reply to Macmillan; she drafted dozens of letters in which she revealed her deepest fears and most frightening thoughts. Afterwards, she invariably felt that she had confessed more than she should have, and tore the letters up. Yet the act of writing them, even without sending them, proved to be a form of therapy in itself. By committing the unspeakable to the page, she was helping to excise it from her mind, even if only temporarily. Jackie eventually asked David Ormsby-Gore to explain to Macmillan the reason for the delay in her reply, and to tell him that the effort of attempting to reply to him had been almost as valuable to her as the advice he had given to her.

Another family friend enlisted by Bobby Kennedy to be of service to Jackie as a counselor and listening ear was a Jesuit priest named Father Richard McSorley. Father McSorley came to visit Jackie in the guise of a tennis coach; in addition to being a priest, he was also an expert tennis player. She was quick to trust him. After only two days of tennis lessons, Jackie was already confiding to McSorley that she had contemplated suicide, and that she longed for death. She posed McSorley with thorny doctrinal questions: if she killed herself, would she, as the Church taught, die in sin and thus be separated from Jack in the afterlife? She prayed for death, and asked McSorley if he would pray for her death as well. He said that he would, if that was what she wanted. "It's not wrong to pray to die," he told her. Yet as their conversations continued, McSorley confided to Bobby Kennedy his fears that Jackie might be suicidal in earnest.

All strong emotion affects the human body on a physiological level, but PTSD specifically wreaks profound changes in the body's production of hormones such as adrenaline and cortisol, which flood the central nervous system when the mind perceives itself to be in mortal peril. The process which the body undergoes in such life-or-death situations is meant to prepare it for survival against impossible odds. Adrenaline makes us faster and strong, quicker to react to threats; cortisol promotes wound healing. Ordinarily, we only experience these adrenaline rushes in brief bursts, and the body's hormone production levels soon return to baseline. But some people who experience severe trauma do not return to baseline for months or years after the traumatic event. Their body and mind remain in what might be called a battle-ready state long after the danger has passed. The effects of sustaining this level of hypervigilance over a long period of time take an enormous toll on the sufferer's mental and physical health. When Jackie told Father McSorley that she felt as though she were "bleeding inside", she was speaking less metaphorically than probably even she realized. She was not merely grieving; she was ill. And every time something happened to remind her of the events of November 22, her illness worsened. Unfortunately, she was nothing if not surrounded by such reminders. From the crowds of mourners that gathered outside her home, to the newspaper headlines and magazine covers that continued to publish front page photographs from Dallas, it seemed at times as if the entire world was determined to make Jackie relive the worst moments of her life.

"My crazy sister-in-law"

Everyone that Jackie was closest to, all of the people she loved most, were giving her advice and counsel along the lines of "time heals all wounds". But this is generally unlikely to be true of people with untreated PTSD, and it certainly wasn't true of Jackie, for whom time brought nothing but more reminders of Dallas and Jack, reminders that triggered sudden, uncontrollable states of sheer desperation. By her own frank assessment, she was still a "walking wound" eight months after November of 1963. She was getting worse, not better, and everyone around her knew it. When she moved from Washington to Manhattan in 1964, she hoped it would prove the start of a new life. Washington is a company town, and Jackie had been married to the head of the company; she could go nowhere without being recognized. In New York, a city of some 7 million people at the time, she hoped to be able to live a comparatively anonymous existence. In accordance with Bobby's suggestion that she was wallowing in her grief to a self-indulgent extent, Jackie blamed herself for her own instability, feeling that it must be some weakness in her character that made it impossible for her to feel normal. By moving away from the city where she had lived most of her married life, she was "making an effort"—that is, taking a decisive step that would hopefully prove to her friends and family that she was doing everything she could to aid her own recovery.

But her anonymity in New York was short lived. The city was the site of Bobby Kennedy's campaign headquarters, as he geared up for his 1964 Senate bid. Likewise, Lyndon Johnson, who was courting Jackie's favor with more enthusiasm than tact, was preparing for re-election (or rather, preparing to be elected for the first time in his own right.) Despite their mutual antipathy for one another, Bobby and Johnson had agreed to endorse one another— Johnson, in the hopes that Bobby would not make a bid for the VP slot during the convention, Bobby, because Johnson held sway with New York politicians who were slow to support his own campaign, viewing him as a mere carpetbagger. Both men made use of Jackie during the campaign, though in Johnson's case, he had to trade favors with her brother in law in order to gain access to her. This quickly put an end to Jackie's anonymous existence in Manhattan. Still, Jackie was for the most part willing to made use of, if it would help get Bobby elected. She, like virtually everyone else, saw Bobby chiefly as an avatar for the spirit of JFK's presidency. "He *must* win," she would say, as though Bobby's victory would confer some measure of immortality on her husband's memory.

Throughout the last four years of RFK's life, he and Jackie were extremely close—closer in some ways than Jackie had ever been to Jack. Their bond was so intense that many people speculated that they were having an affair, though there was no basis to the rumors. Jackie relied on Bobby in everything, while Bobby, though he cared deeply and genuinely for Jackie, could never quite leave politics out of their relationship. (Though for a man who hoped to become president in 1968, this was undoubtedly true of all his relationships.) When he campaigned for his Senate seat in New York, it was Jackie he wanted with him, and Jackie's children, rather than Ethel or any of his own plentiful brood of children. Bobby sometimes felt resentful of the fact that his entire career was predicated on the premise that he was carrying on with the work begun by his brother—seeing the giant crowds that had amassed to greet him at one campaign stop, he muttered to an aide, "They're here for him, not me"—but he was too pragmatic not to derive as much advantage as possible from evoking Jack's legacy. And since no one evoked Jack's legacy like Jackie did, he had to make use of her.

Only once did Jackie and Bobby's relationship erupt into tension and resentment, and when it did so, the fault lay with Jackie—or rather, with Jackie's post-traumatic stress. Sometimes, when she had a triggering experience, her outward reactions were almost beyond her control, and since the trigger was not always apparent to onlookers, her behavior on these occasions could seem wild, irrational, and utterly bewildering.

Secretary of Defense Robert McNamara, who was probably Jackie's closest friend after Bobby, once unwittingly provoked an outburst from Jackie that baffled him for years. As the principle architect of the war in Vietnam, McNamara suffered many sleepless nights, struggling to reconcile his belief in the possibility of victory and regime change with the enormous toll that was being exacted in human suffering. He often turned to Jackie for companionship and comfort, because he could not bring himself to confide his doubts to his wife and children, who were uncomfortable with his role in the conflict overseas. One night, as Jackie and McNamara were discussing a poem which described a woman's tormented passion for an unfaithful lover, Jackie suddenly went silent and glassy-eyed, then turned to McNamara and began screaming, hitting his chest, demanding that he put an end to the bloodshed in Vietnam.

McNamara was stunned and confused by the suddenness with which she had turned on him. But in retrospect, the likeliest explanation for Jackie's outburst was that the poem had reminded her of Jack's faithlessness in their marriage. Thoughts of Jack had triggered flashbacks of the assassination, and the memory of cradling her husband's shattered skull in her hands had in turn filled her with overwhelming rage at the knowledge that so much senseless violence was being inflicted on (and by) American soldiers halfway around the world. Besides Lyndon Johnson, no single individual was more responsible for the war in Vietnam than McNamara—hence, his unluckily becoming the focus of Jackie's sudden, seemingly inexplicable fury.

Episodes of this nature, in which Jackie reacted wildly to triggers that others did not perceive, had caused Bobby to once refer to Jackie as "my crazy sister-in-law". But he himself had never been the hapless target of such an outburst from her—at least, not until 1967, when *Look* magazine began publishing excerpts from William Manchester's upcoming book, *The Death of a President*. Shortly after the assassination, in the awareness that historians and journalists would waste little time in producing the first biographies of John F. Kennedy, Jackie had sought to exercise as much control over her husband's biographical narrative as possible. Every would-be Kennedy biographer naturally coveted the blessing and cooperation of Kennedy's widow. Arthur Schlesinger, the so-called "court historian" of Kennedy's administration, had persuaded Jackie to take part in an oral history project not long after the assassination, interviewing her for hours about every aspect of her life with Kennedy while a tape recorder ran in the background. It was important, he had felt, that Jackie make her contribution to the historical record in this way, as she had been the foremost spectator to one of the most important events of the 20th century. Jackie agreed to participate on the condition that she would have the final authority to review the transcripts of the tapes and strike from the record anything she did not want other people to read. Parts of the the transcripts would be sealed until after her death.

Schlesinger, who had written biographies of Franklin D. Roosevelt and Harry Truman, and was the foremost authority on the rise of mid-century American liberalism, felt that he was the natural choice to write the definitive biography of JFK's life. The oral history recordings Jackie had provided him with would be one of his most important sources for that book. But Jackie was unhappy with the fact that Schlesinger, who felt that he had an ethical obligation as a historian to pursue truth over tact, would not allow the Kennedy family—that is, herself and Bobby—to have editorial rights over the manuscript. Jackie was deeply uncomfortable with this, realizing that she had confessed more to Schlesinger during their interview sessions than she necessarily wanted the world to know. She preferred the arrangement she had made with William Manchester, who was contractually obligated to give both Jackie and Bobby vetting rights over the final version of his book.

Manchester had not jockeyed for the privilege of being Kennedy's authorized biographer. On the contrary, Jackie had sought him out for the role, on the basis of the fact that Manchester had written an earlier book about Kennedy's campaign that portrayed the president in a flattering light. More importantly, he had sent the manuscript to the White House ahead of publication, inviting Kennedy to review his own quotes and make changes to them, if he wished. This deferential attitude was what made Jackie choose him for the honor of writing her husband's definitive, authorized biography—and when Manchester agreed in writing to give her and Bobby the right to make amendments to his manuscript, the wisdom of her choice seemed to be confirmed.

There was just one problem. Though it had been Jackie who sought Manchester out to offer him this opportunity, she proved maddeningly difficult to work with. Manchester offered to drop everything and fly out at any time that was convenient to her in order to conduct interviews for the book. But Jackie put him off for months before she finally consented to see him—and even then, on their first meeting, she had to turn him away practically at the front door, because she found herself too overcome with dread to proceed any further that day. Manchester did manage to conduct a few interviews with Jackie, but even though she spoke incessantly of the assassination to her close friends and family, she found that dredging the memories up on command for Manchester's benefit was making her already precarious mental health even worse. After a few weeks of interviews, she abruptly cut him off, arranging for all of Manchester's future inquiries to go through Bobby, who ensured that he was handed off to aides who had been instructed to stall him indefinitely. For good reason, Manchester found all of this incredibly frustrating. But that was nothing compared to what happened when the book was finally completed and ready to go to press.

Manchester, himself a veteran of World War II who had undergone severe battlefield trauma in Okinawa, found writing *The Death of a President* to be a grueling, even debilitating task. Ironically, the same kind of post-traumatic stress that made it so difficult for Jackie to speak with him was triggered in Manchester himself as he obsessively recreated the events of November 22, 1963, in his mind and on the page. He was hospitalized for nervous exhaustion shortly before completing the book, and in fact wrote the final chapters while still in the hospital. On one occasion, the anxiety induced by writing about the assassination made him grip his pen so tightly that it broke and cut his thumb. Finishing the book and seeing it go to print became an obsession with him, even though he had never sought to write it in the first place. When Manchester turned the final draft over to Bobby Kennedy for approval, as his contract stipulated, Bobby returned it, mostly unedited, with his blessing to go ahead with publication. Even though the approval of both Bobby and Jackie was required by the contract, Bobby did not send the manuscript on to Jackie for her approval. After all, she had been ignoring Manchester's letters and requests for meetings for months. Bobby assumed, quite reasonably, that the last thing Jackie would want was to relive the events of Dallas yet again by editing Manchester's book herself.

The assumption was understandable, but it was drastically mistaken. Jackie only learned that *The Death of a President* was slated for publication when Bobby informed her that *Look* magazine had purchased the serialization rights, and that the first edition was due to come out the following month. Jackie was disbelieving at first, then furious. Suddenly, Bobby found himself on the receiving end of one of Jackie's seemingly inexplicable fits of narrowly targeted rage. In all probability, Jackie was not angered by the fact that Bobby had authorized the book's publication without running it past her first so much as she felt frightened and helpless in the face of the realization that, once again, everywhere she went, the front pages of newspapers and covers of magazines would be plastered with images from Dallas.

When she had first approached Manchester about writing the book, she expressed the opinion that, while an official biography of Kennedy must be written, it ought to be consigned to some dark library shelf immediately after publication. She wasn't entirely serious about that, but she hadn't anticipated magazine serialization either. She'd contracted Manchester to write Kennedy's biography shortly after the events of Dallas, at a time when she couldn't possibly have anticipated how long the American public would remain obsessed with the assassination. But in the years that had followed, she'd grown to loathe the

November 22 anniversary, as new articles and stories and headlines cropped up like perennial plants, dragging her back into the past. For the rest of her life, she would refer to November and December as her difficult time of the year, a period for retreat and reclusiveness, during which she was careful never to commit to any public appearances. The stoic widow in the black veil had been an illusion. She had not cried during the funeral because she was simply too numb. Nowadays, triggering incidents could produce weeping fits that lasted for hours. The last thing she wanted was to appear in public in such a state.

Dreading the deluge of publicity that would come about as a result of the book's serialization, Jackie demanded that Bobby rescind his approval and find a way to put a halt to the publication of *The Death of a President*. It was not a rational request, and Bobby's reluctant agreement was not a rational decision on his part. The lawsuit that followed, which was ultimately unsuccessful in preventing the book from being published, damaged both of them in the eyes of the public. Ever since the assassination, Jackie had been placed on a pedestal, above criticism. Now, journalists began to express the opinion that it was time for a reassessment of the former First Lady's status. Her obsessive grief, her desperate attempts to shield herself from reminders of her husband's death, which was now playing out in lawsuits and newspaper headlines, was accomplishing nothing more than to drag the country back into the past, the articles said.

What the journalists did not realize was that Jackie's nightmare—her conviction that Jack's death was not a unique event, but rather the opening salvo of more violence yet to come—was far from baseless. Her intuition was about to be proven horrifyingly prescient. The summer of 1968 was about to demonstrate to America, and to the world, that the Kennedy assassination had inaugurated a new age of public violence and assault on public figures, such as the world had never seen before.

Chapter Six: 1968

The assassination of Martin Luther King, Jr.

For Jackie Kennedy, all sense of permanent safety in ordinary existence had been eradicated the day of her husband's assassination. The impossible had happened once, in Dallas in 1963. As far as she was concerned, the rules of ordinary life had been suspended since that moment, and she now lived in a world where worst-case scenarios were now as likely to occur as anything else. This became startlingly apparent to her sister's close friend, society photographer Cecil Beaton, who accompanied Jackie to a performance of the New York City Ballet in February of 1968. When a prop gun was fired, the sound virtually indistinguishable from that of a real gun, Jackie "nearly [jumped] out of her seat and over the rail of the dress circle". Scarcely an instant had passed between the crack of the blank being fired and Jackie's reacting to it. She was prepared, at all times, for the world to come crashing down on her again. To her friends and loved ones, especially Bobby, this was just another demonstration of Jackie behaving like his "crazy sister-in-law". But after the spring of 1968 gave way to summer, Jackie's "craziness" would soon be shared by most of the country, as one wave of devastating violence precipitated another—all of it taking place against the backdrop of the Vietnam War, the bloody footage of which was being broadcast on TV in American homes every night.

In early 1968, all of Bobby Kennedy's energy was focused on his upcoming bid to supplant Lyndon Johnson on the ticket at the Democratic convention that summer. He had finally succeeded in articulating a personal political platform that was distinct from his brother's, without rejecting any part of the all-valuable Kennedy legacy that Bobby purported to be upholding. He favored de-escalation of American involvement in Vietnam, and a stronger emphasis on civil rights than Jack Kennedy had managed to find room for in his own domestic policy. As such, he was seen, much as Jack had been, as the fresh face of a new generation of young voters who were rejecting the hawkish values of their elders. Bobby's chances of victory seemed strong; Lyndon Johnson had chosen not to seek re-election after being soundly defeated by Eugene McCarthy in the New Hampshire primary. The summer progressed, and Bobby Kennedy seemed poised to carry all before him. But though Jackie gave Bobby's candidacy her wholehearted support, she was plagued with forebodings about his safety. "Do you know what I think will happen to Bobby if he is elected president?" she asked Arthur Schlesinger in April of 1968. "The same thing that happened to Jack. There is so much hatred in this country, and more people hate Bobby than hated Jack. That's why I don't want him to be president."

Jackie wasn't the only person who feared that Bobby Kennedy would meet Jack's fate. His own aides were constantly urging him to take precautions that Bobby rejected—much as Jack had rejected precautions in Dallas, such as a bulletproof bubbletop covering for the open limousine.

Then, on April 4, 1968, the assassination of revered civil rights leader Martin Luther King, Jr. in Memphis, Tennessee, triggered an explosion of protests and violence in cities across the United States. It was as if Jackie's conviction that all the old rules of civilized society had been suspended were suddenly being confirmed. As one biographer writes: "The nation that had recently chided Jackie to let Americans put the past behind them was suddenly, ineluctably, hurled back into that very past, as commentators linked the civil rights leader's murder to the assassination of President Kennedy." It had been four and a half years since Dallas, yet suddenly it was as if no time at all had gone by. Even Bobby Kennedy, who had had long felt that Jackie's attitude after the assassination bordered on hysterical over-reaction, began to feel that perhaps, after all, Jack's death really had "set something loose in this country."

Jackie, naturally, empathized deeply with Coretta Scott King, who, she felt, was perhaps better positioned than anyone else in the country to understand Jackie's own suffering—although at least Mrs. King had the comfort of knowing that her husband had died for a noble cause, a comfort Jackie envied. The results of the Warren Commission, which had conducted a lengthy investigation into the Kennedy assassination, had ultimately concluded that Oswald had acted alone from no discernible political or ideological motive. This was a disappointment to Jackie, who would have derived more consolation from knowing that her husband had died for his beliefs, rather than in an act of senseless violence. Jackie released a rare public statement of support for King's widow: "When will our country learn that to live by the sword is to perish by the sword? I pray that with the price he paid—his life—he will make room in people's hearts for love, not hate. Some people would never kill—but even to speak of another with hatred is the same and causes death." Though it was increasingly uncommon for Jackie to make public appearances, and it was especially difficult for her to make an appearance in conjunction with such a violent and tragic event, she decided to attend MLK's funeral in Atlanta after Coretta Scott King told Bobby Kennedy, who was already planning to walk in King's funeral procession, that she thought Jackie's presence "would indeed count for a great deal".

After the funeral, Jackie remarked that the public's sympathy for Coretta Scott King and her family would soon turn to impatience, as had happened with her. "Of course people feel guilty for a moment," she told Schlesinger. "But they hate feeling guilty. They can't stand it for very long. They turn."

The assassination of RFK

By May of 1968, Bobby Kennedy's presidential campaign was gaining serious momentum. After winning the Indiana and Nebraska primaries in May, all that remained was Oregon and California. McCarthy won Oregon on May 28; Bobby determined that, unless he won California, he would drop out of the race and save his energies for the 1972 election. As Bobby's star continued to rise, however, Jackie's fears for him increased. The King assassination had only cemented her belief that Bobby had a target on his back, a concern shared by many of those close to him. But, if anything, Bobby was even more contemptuous of the danger than he had been before King's death. Just as Jack Kennedy's conviction that he would not live past middle age had conferred a certain reckless upon him, the deaths of JFK and King seemed to fuel Bobby's determination to push on relentlessly, whatever the danger.

Jackie did not join Bobby on the campaign trail during his nomination bid, but she monitored his progress closely. Despite her fears for his safety should he be elected president, she wanted him to win, and she knew that the June 4th California primary would make or break his chances. She was in her apartment in New York when she received news of Bobby's victory in California. Due to the three-hour time difference between the east and west coast, she was in bed when Bobby made his victory speech. But she awakened promptly, four hours later, when her bedside telephone rang. It was her sister's husband, Stas Radziwill, calling from England, and the start of their conversation ran as follows:

"Isn't it wonderful?" said Jackie immediately. "He's won. He's got California."

"But how is he?" said Stas.

"Oh, he's fine. He's won."
"But how is he?"

"What do you mean?"

At that point, Radziwill found himself tasked with the unenviable job of explaining to Jackie that Bobby had been shot in the head while leaving the Ambassador Hotel through the kitchen exit. He was still alive, but severely brain damaged. Jackie instantly flew to Los Angeles, where she found Ethel Kennedy sitting next to Bobby's bed, holding his hand, the way Jackie had once sat next to Jack's bed, holding onto him even after doctors draped his head with a sheet. Teddy Kennedy, then a 36-year old junior senator from Massachusetts, was kneeling at the foot of the bed, praying. It was all too sickeningly familiar, all too reminiscent of Dallas. Yet Jackie had retreated into the same blessedly numb state which had enabled her to go through the motions back in November of 1963.

She remained by Bobby's bedside until he was at last pronounced dead, 26 hours later. Lyndon Johnson promptly sent a presidential jet to Los Angeles to transport Bobby and his family to New York, where his requiem mass would be celebrated. Everyone, especially Jackie, was overwhelmed by memories of Dallas; everything about the day felt so similar to November 22 that it was if the nightmare of the past which had plagued Jackie for so long had finally enveloped everyone else as well. As one biographer writes: "What did it mean any longer for Bobby to have called Jackie his crazy sister-in-law when so many other people—sane, reasonable, responsible people—suddenly share her sense of dread?" It was if the floodgates had been opened and some strain of madness that had long been buried in the American psyche was affecting people en masse. The world had changed irrevocably. Jackie's characterization of Jack Kennedy's administration as a fairy tale era in the tradition of ancient Camelot no longer struck people as excessively sentimental. It seemed that America had been a more innocent nation when Jack was alive. Now, no one was quite certain what sort of world it was they were living in anymore.

Jackie Kennedy Onassis

The effect that Bobby's death had on Jackie can scarcely be overestimated. Not only did his assassination leave her bereft of the man who had been a figure of vital emotional support in her life ever since he raced to her bedside after the stillbirth of her daughter Arabella in 1956, but his death convinced her that she, or her children, would be the next high-profile figure to be targeted by a mad gunman. Whatever tentative progress she had made in her recovery from Jack's death threatened to be undone by this latest tragedy. Her sister, Lee Radziwill, anticipated a new decline in Jackie's mental health with dread. "You don't know what it's like being with Jackie," Lee complained to Cecil Beaton. "She's really more than half around the bend. She can't sleep at night, she can't stop thinking about herself and never feeling anything but sorry for herself. 'I'm so unprotected,' she says. But she is surrounded by friends, helpers, FBI...She takes no interest in anything for more than two minutes. She rushes around paying visits but won't settle down anywhere or to anything. She can't love anyone... The new horror will bring the old one alive again and I'm going to have to go through hell trying to calm her."

Was it any wonder that Jackie doubted the capacity of her Secret Service agents to protect her? After all, Jack and Bobby both had protection details much larger than hers, and that had not saved them. It was true that she had more people surrounding her, dedicated to her well-being, than most people who were not wealthy former First Ladies. But she was also the most famous woman in the world, which made her vulnerable in a way that most people could not possibly comprehend.

Lee was right that "the new horror" had brought "the old one alive again". But contrary to the rest of Lee's assumptions, Jackie's response to RFK's death, while undoubtedly a result of her post-traumatic stress disorder, did not take the form of wild outbursts of uncontrolled emotion. She didn't have time for that. Perceiving herself, not irrationally, to be in danger, all her instincts were geared towards survival. "If they're killing Kennedys, then my children are targets," she said. "I want to get out of this country." Once committed to this course of action, she quickly found the path to security she was looking for in the form of an old family friend: Aristotle Onassis.

Jackie had first met Onassis in 1958. Fabulously wealthy, devoted to collecting illustrious acquaintances who could heighten his social cachet and legitimize his image, he had hosted a gathering aboard his yacht the *Christina* to honor aging British prime minister Winston Churchill. Jack Kennedy, for whom Churchill had long been a personal hero, had attended the gathering with Jackie in hopes of meeting him. Jack had been disappointed to find that Churchill's ailing health made any kind of meaningful conversation with him impossible. But Onassis remained a fixture in the Kennedys' life from that point forward. In 1963, after the death of her infant son Patrick, Jackie had spent three months cruising the Aegean, a holiday she deeply regretted having taken when Jack died two months after her return. The cruise had taken place aboard the *Christina,* with Onassis acting as her host. She had next seen Onassis at Jack's funeral, and his behavior towards Jackie during her mourning year was described as "beautiful".

Now, in the wake of the RFK assassination, Onassis appeared on the scene again, this time with an agenda. He wanted Jackie to be his wife. Years earlier, he had divorced his first wife, the mother of his two children, in order to pursue a relationship with legendary opera singer Maria Callas. But now he spotted an opportunity to win the hand of the most famous woman in the world. He seemed to sense that in the wake of Bobby's death, Jackie was terrified for her safety. He also knew that she was well aware how much protection he was in a position to offer her. Onassis owned his own private island, his own private airline, a yacht the size of a warship, and a private security force of around seventy men. He was also heavily involved with the so-called "Regime of the Colonels", the Greek military junta which had seized control of the country in 1967, and was on the verge of gaining exclusive government contracts that would greatly increase his personal wealth. Marriage to a woman with the unparalleled social cachet of Mrs. John F. Kennedy would only make those negotiations easier.

Onassis courted Jackie, and indeed her entire family, in ostentatious fashion. He was alive to the fact that there would be strenuous objections from Jackie's loved ones to their marriage, so he labored mightily to win them over, lest they persuade Jackie to reject him. Jackie, Rose Kennedy, and Janet Auchincloss all found themselves showered in gifts of fabulously expensive jewelry—Jackie's collection of such trinkets alone was valued in the millions. Teddy, the sole surviving brother and youngest of all the

Kennedy children, who now found himself thrust unwillingly into Bobby's shoes as head of the family, was assigned to dissuade Jackie from the marriage if possible, but Onassis plied him with alcohol and pretty girls until Teddy, too, was under his sway.

Onassis was 23 years Jackie's senior, divorced with a former wife still living (which meant that marrying him might put Jackie in danger of being excommunicated from the Catholic church), and was viewed by many as an enemy of the United States. Apart from being a wealthy womanizer, he was the opposite of Jack Kennedy in every way. There was outcry not only from Jackie's family, but from the American press. Accused of being a fortune hunter, and of abandoning her duty to the nation to marry a wealthy foreign criminal, Jackie was not merely swept off her pedestal—the pedestal itself was smashed to rubble. But Jackie was unmoved. When Bunny Mellon, one of her oldest friends since before her White House days, asked Jackie why she was marrying Onassis, Jackie made no attempt to persuade her that she had fallen in love. "I have no choice," she said. "They're playing Ten Little Indians," she said, referring to the 1965 movie in which ten party guests are invited to a mysterious mansion, where they are murdered one by one. "I don't want to be next."

In marrying Onassis, Jackie stood to forfeit her right to a Secret Service protection detail and the three million dollar Kennedy trust fund which had been established for her. It seemed a fair price to pay in exchange for what Ari could offer her. Whether or not she was, truly, safer as the wife of a man who was hated the world over, whose close ties to Greece's military dictatorship could easily one day sweep him into a maelstrom of political instability, mattered less than the fact that Onassis had successfully sold her the image of absolute security, and a luxurious, private existence in which what Jackie referred to as "the outside world" could be held at bay. Jackie made one final appearance in the U.S. as Mrs. John F. Kennedy to attend the commissioning ceremony for the Naval aircraft carrier which was to be named in Jack's honor. Then, on October 20, 1968, in a Greek Orthodox ceremony attended by only a few of the bride and groom's closest family members, she became Mrs. Aristotle Onassis— or, as the tabloids would dub her in later years, "Jackie O."

The headlines in the American newspapers were positively histrionic. From "Jackie, Why?" to "Jack Kennedy Dies Today for a Second Time", there wasn't a journalist in the country who had a positive word to say about her marriage. But Jackie believed wholeheartedly that Jack Kennedy, looking down from heaven at the state of the world in which he had left her to make her way without him, understood her decision. In fact, she believed that it was what he would want for her, and for their children. She had upheld her duty to Jack's memory to the very best of her ability for the last five years, working diligently to preserve his legacy and ensure that he was remembered the way that she believed he would wish to be remembered. All that remained now was for her to ensure that their children grew up safe and cared for—and Onassis, she believed, was the one man on earth who could make that possible for her. As she wrote to Secret Service director James Rowley shortly before her marriage: "The children will never be safer than they will be on Skorpios [Onassis's private island] or the *Christina*...As the person in the world who is most interested in their security, and who recognizes most what threats there are in the outside world, I promise you that I have considered and tried every way, and that what I ask you for is what I know is best for the children of President Kennedy and what he would wish for them." In the end, John and Caroline retained their Secret Service details, but Onassis remained the person in whom Jackie placed all her hopes for their safety.

Jackie's marriage to Aristotle Onassis began as a kind of fairy tale, at least in her eyes, but it remained that way for only a short time. In surrendering her image as the chaste, almost saintly window of the slain President, Jackie found herself laid bare to a media industry that no one longer felt obligated to treat her with any respect or deference. She began to be pursued by paparazzi whenever she was in New York, where John and Caroline attended school. After the paparazzi began infiltrating their way past Onassis's private security force on Skorpios, Jackie grew disillusioned with the image of Onassis as an all-powerful protector. Likewise, Onassis, who had believed that his marriage to Jackie would open doors to lucrative business deals in the U.S., only to find that this was not the case, grew disillusioned with her, and began to be seen once again with his previous lover, Maria Callas. Jackie began to spend most of her time in New York with John and Caroline, where she saw Onassis only infrequently. Yet she continued to feel great affection towards him, for "rescuing" her "at a moment when my life was engulfed in shadows". Likewise, Onassis continued to treat her, and John and Caroline, extremely well.

In 1973, however, Onassis's beloved son Alexander, who had never liked Jackie nor approved of his father's marrying her, was critically injured in a plane crash and died soon afterwards. The death left Onassis a broken man, and many people in Greece, most notably his daughter Christina, blamed Jackie for it—not because of anything she had done, but because they believed, sincerely, that Jackie was cursed, and that she had spread that curse to the Onassis family when she married into it. After several other misfortunes befell the family, including the death of Alexander and Christina's mother, the increasingly unreasonable Onassis began to blame Jackie as well. He made arrangements for divorce proceedings—only to abandon them when he was diagnosed with a neuromuscular disease that would prove fatal in a few months' time. Aristotle Onassis died in Paris on March 15, 1975, leaving Jackie Kennedy Onassis a widow for the second time at the age of forty-five.

Over the course of the next nineteen years, before her death on May 19, 1994, at the age of 64, Jackie slowly began to gain the one thing that had been denied her in her otherwise privileged existence. She grew to feel in control of her own life in a way she never had before. Shortly after Onassis died, she went to work as an editor for Viking publishing house, the first "real" job she'd had since she worked as an "Inquiring Camera Girl" for the *Times-Herald* in the early 1950's. She began seeing a therapist as well, for the first time in her life. When the war in Vietnam came to a close, and thousands of American veterans returned home carrying the psychological and emotional damage of their combat experiences, psychologists began to study the effects of prolonged trauma in earnest, which, even if it did not lead to increased public understand of Jackie's suffering, may have contributed to the success of her therapy. It was not that her new existence was free from danger and threat—indeed, in 1975, Caroline, who was studying in London, nearly fell victim to an IRA car bomb explosion intended for a different victim. The close call naturally left Jackie feeling badly shaken.

But Jackie, who had grown up in an era where girls were brought up to order their entire existence around their husbands, was, for the very first time in her life, relying solely on herself, and not on any man. Control, agency, empowerment—all of these things are essential to recovery from post-traumatic stress disorder. By October of 1980, Jackie felt a strong enough sense of well-being that, when she was asked at a dinner party what she considered to be the greatest achievement of her life thus far, she replied, "I think it is that after going through a rather difficult time, I consider myself comparatively sane. I am proud of that."

Other great books by Michael W. Simmons on Kindle, paperback and audio:

Elizabeth I: Legendary Queen Of England

Alexander Hamilton: First Architect Of The American Government

William Shakespeare: An Intimate Look Into The Life Of The Most Brilliant Writer In The History Of The English Language

Thomas Edison: American Inventor

Catherine the Great: Last Empress of Russia

Romanov: The Last Tsarist Dynasty

Peter the Great: Autocrat and Reformer

The Rothschilds: The Dynasty and the Legacy

Queen Victoria: Icon of an Era

Six Wives: The Women Who Married, Lived, and
Died for Henry VIII

John D. Rockefeller: The Wealthiest Man in
American History

Princess to Queen: The Early Years of Queen
Elizabeth II

Queen of People's Hearts: The Life and Mission
of Diana, Princess of Wales

Further Reading

Jacqueline Bouvier Kennedy Onassis: The Untold Story, by Barbara Leaming

Obituary of Jacqueline Kennedy Onassis, New York Times

http://www.nytimes.com/learning/general/onthisday/bday/0728.html

Official biography of Jacqueline Kennedy Onassis, Kennedy Presidential Library

https://www.jfklibrary.org/JFK/Life-of-Jacqueline-B-Kennedy.aspx

Theodore White interview with Jacqueline Kennedy, Kennedy Presidential Library

https://www.jfklibrary.org/Asset-Viewer/Archives/THWPP-059-009.aspx

"The Legacy of John F. Kennedy", by Alan Brinkley

https://www.theatlantic.com/magazine/archive/2013/08/the-legacy-of-john-f-kennedy/309499/

Made in the USA
Las Vegas, NV
27 May 2023